Vita-Mix®

COOKBOOK

Vita-Mix®

COOKBOOK

'WELCOME TO THE WORLD OF VITA-MIX'

DUNCAN BAIRD PUBLISHERS

LONDON

Vita-Mix® COOKBOOK

Copyright © Vita-Mix® Corporation 2009
Text copyright © Vita-Mix® Corporation 2009
Photography copyright © Vita-Mix® Corporation 2009

Created and designed for Vita-Mix Corporation by Duncan Baird Publishers

First published in the United Kingdom and Ireland in 2009 for Vita-Mix Corporation by
Duncan Baird Publishers Ltd
Sixth Floor, Castle House
75–76 Wells Street
London W1T 3QH

Managing Editor: Grace Cheetham
Editor: Nicole Bator
Managing Designer: Suzanne Tuhrim
Designer: Jantje Doughty
Commissioned photography: Simon Smith and Toby Scott; additional photography by Ian O'Leary
  (pp 29, 54, 64, 114, 134) and Nic Wingate (p 8)
Food Stylist: Mari Mererid Williams; additional food styling by Gizzi Erskine (pp 29, 54, 64, 114, 134)
Prop Stylist: Rachel Jukes; additional prop styling by Paul Reid (pp 29, 54, 64, 114, 134)
Recipes by Paula Bartimeus and Christine Bailey

British Library Cataloguing-in-Publication Data:
A CIP record for this book is available from the British Library

ISBN: 978-1-84483-857-8

10 9 8 7 6 5 4 3 2 1

Typeset in Frutiger
Colour reproduction by imagewrite
Printed in Singapore by Imago

Publisher's Note: While every care has been taken in compiling the recipes for this book, Vita-Mix Corporation, or any other persons who have been involved in working on this publication, cannot accept responsibility for any errors or omissions, inadvertent or not, that may be found in the recipes or text, nor for any problems that may arise as a result of preparing one of these recipes. If you are pregnant or breastfeeding or have any special dietary requirements or medical conditions, it is advisable to consult a medical professional before following any of the recipes contained in this book. Ill or elderly people, babies, young children and women who are pregnant or breastfeeding should avoid the recipes containing uncooked eggs or raw meat or fish.

Notes on the Recipes
Unless otherwise stated:
• Use medium eggs, fruit and vegetables
• Use fresh ingredients, including herbs and chillies
• Do not mix metric and imperial measurements
• 1 tsp = 5ml
  1 tbsp = 15ml
  1 cup = 250ml

Contents

Introduction

Welcome to the wonderful world of Vita-Mix® – unquestionably the best kitchen appliance you can own.

The Vita-Mix machine is not just a food processor, it's so much more. From blending, juicing, shredding and grinding to cooking, melting and freezing, the Vita-Mix machine reduces or eliminates the need for other kitchen appliances. In fact this one amazing piece of equipment does the work of 10 without a single attachment! So in a matter of minutes or even seconds, you can have delicious juices, smoothies, sauces, dips, spreads, purées, dressings, soups, ice creams, salads and baby foods, making short work of numerous difficult, time-consuming kitchen tasks.

But it's not just the wide range of food preparations it can be used for that makes the Vita-Mix machine so unique. The machine really is an investment in health. Driving the Vita-Mix machine is a motor so powerful it is far more than you will need to handle even the most difficult processes. Its stainless steel blades can rotate up to an astounding 240 miles (385 kilometres) per hour, so that whole foods aren't just blended: they're pulverized down to a cellular level. This allows locked-in nutrients and disease-fighting antioxidants that are trapped within the cell walls of fresh fruit and vegetables to be released, making them more bio-available and easier for the body to absorb. Breakthrough research from the University of Toronto in Ontario, Canada shows that processing with the Vita-Mix machine may significantly enhance nutrient intake from whole foods. The results of this 2008 study clearly indicate that the Vita-Mix machine has the ability to disrupt plant cell wall structure and reduce food particle size considerably, which may enhance the bio-availability of essential nutrients in fruits and vegetables.

The Vita-Mix blades rotate so fast on high speed that if left on long enough the friction that's produced creates enough heat to cook raw vegetable soups in 4–8 minutes. This means more flavour and less nutrient loss compared to conventional cooking methods.

Amazingly, healthy frozen treats (both dairy-based and non-dairy) can also be prepared in the same machine. The Vita-Mix machine's high-performance cutting blades crush frozen fruit and ice efficiently, releasing coldness and causing mixtures to refreeze, so you can enjoy guilt-free homemade ice creams in a matter of seconds.

You may think that the Vita-Mix machine, with its diverse range of functions and super-advanced technology, is a recent invention, but it's been around for quite a while: the first model was introduced in the United States in 1937 by founder W G ('Papa') Barnard, a self-taught salesman of 'modern' home products. As television entered the mainstream in the 1940s, 'Papa' Barnard's son Bill immediately recognized this new medium as the perfect way to showcase a new and improved version of the Vita-Mix machine, and it wasn't long before it became a household name across the country.

In 1969, with Bill's son Grover on board, the Vita-Mix 3600 (and later 4000) truly revolutionized what could be done in a blender, with the large motor and friction-cooking capability enabling it to freeze and dispense solid ice cream, grind grain, cook soup and make a creamy, smooth, total juice from whole fruits and vegetables. Further research and testing resulted in a super-powerful, improved Vita-Mix machine introduced in 1992. It's a machine about which 'Papa' Barnard could only have dreamed. Now under the direction of the third and fourth generations of the Barnard family, Vita-Mix Corporation distributes its products in more than 80 countries.

Built to last a lifetime, the Vita-Mix machine will revolutionize the way you cook and prepare food, saving you time and money, and encouraging you to eat for optimum nutrition. In addition, the machine is easy to use (and to clean!), and makes cooking fun and exciting. The 200 mouthwatering recipes in this book will help you get started with everything from quick and easy juices, smoothies and hot soups to sensational sauces, lunches and dinners to decadent desserts, ice creams and sorbets. Choose from a selection of recipes for special occasions, as well as dishes tailored specifically for the babies and toddlers in your life. Using your Vita-Mix machine will soon become an essential part of your daily routine.

Below left: Vita-Mix world headquarters, Ohio, USA; **below right:** *The Vita-Mix machine in action at a UK trade fair.*

THE VITA-MIX MACHINE ABCs

Some exciting things are about to happen in your kitchen! But before you begin preparing food and cooking in your Vita-Mix machine, it's important to familiarize yourself with the product, what it can do and how to use it.

THE CONTAINER

The Vita-Mix container that houses the blades is clearly marked with millilitre, ounce and cup measurements. It's available in two sizes: 2l/64fl oz and 950ml/32oz. The standard 2-litre container is suitable for all your Vita-Mix machine preparations, while the smaller 32-ounce version is ideal for simple kitchen prep work and for making smaller servings.

TWO-PART LID

The 2-part lid is easy to put on and take off and should always be locked in place when the machine is in operation. The lid plug, which fits into the top of the 2-part lid, must also be fitted during processing, but can be removed when adding food or using the tamper.

CONTROL PANEL (HINTS FOR SETTING SPEEDS)

The Vita-Mix machine has an ON/OFF switch, a VARIABLE/HIGH speed switch and a variable speed dial.

- The ON/OFF switch turns the machine on and off.
- Use VARIABLE speed to start off with most mixtures (before turning quickly to HIGH), and for stirring, chopping, shredding and grinding. This setting is required to use the variable-speed dial, which has 10 speed options. Use VARIABLE speeds cautiously as blending too long on too low a speed can overheat the machine and cause the Automatic Overload Protection to turn the machine off.
- Use HIGH speed for making whole-food juices, smoothies, soups, sauces, frozen mixtures and purées. It provides the best quality of refinement, breaking down grains, ice, frozen fruit and whole fruits and vegetables to a smooth lump-free consistency. Turning the machine to HIGH overrides the VARIABLE speed dial and is the fastest speed available.

THE TAMPER

The tamper is a contoured plastic tool that allows you to process very thick and/or frozen mixtures that cannot be processed in a regular blender. Using it maintains circulation by preventing air pockets from forming. While the machine is running, use the tamper to push ingredients into the blades as you make frozen desserts, nut butters or puréed fruits and vegetables. The tamper must only be used with the 2-part lid in place and the lid plug removed.

CARE AND CLEANING

One thing that often puts people off using a juice extractor is the laborious job of cleaning it afterwards. Cleaning the Vita-Mix machine, however, couldn't be easier – it cleans itself in seconds with a drop of soap in some water! Just fill the Vita-Mix container half full with warm water and add one or two drops of washing-up liquid. Secure the 2-part lid and run on HIGH for 30–60 seconds. Turn the machine off, rinse the container and drain. For maintenance reasons, always clean your Vita-Mix machine immediately after use.

HOW TO OPERATE THE VITA-MIX MACHINE

1 Before using your Vita-Mix machine for the first time, clean it thoroughly (as described above).

2 Set the container on the motor base by aligning it over the centring pad.

3 Put soft foods and liquids in the container first; add solid items and ice last.

4 Always use the 2-part lid when blending. The lid plug should only be removed when adding ingredients or when inserting the tamper. When blending hot ingredients, make sure that the lid is securely latched.

5 Select the desired speed. Many foods are blended on HIGH speed. It is recommended that all mixtures requiring HIGH speed should be started on VARIABLE speed 1, quickly increased to VARIABLE speed 10 and then switched to HIGH. If the mixture stops circulating, you have probably trapped an air bubble. If inserting the tamper through the lid plug opening while blending does not release it, reduce the speed and continue to use the tamper in the same way until the mixture 'burps'. If these methods do not work, stop the machine, remove the container from the motor base and use a rubber spatula to press the air bubble away from the blades, then continue to process as before.

6 Until you are accustomed to the machine, pay careful attention to the times given in the recipes to avoid over-processing. Due to the machine's speed, processing times are much quicker than standard appliances.

7 After turning the machine off, wait until the blades stop completely before taking the lid off or removing the container from the motor base.

Note: The Vita-Mix machine is equipped with an Automatic Overload Protection, which protects the motor from overheating. If the mixture you are processing is being run on an inappropriate speed for a longer time than recommended, the Automatic Overload Protection may cause the machine to shut off and possibly emit a faint odour. Do not be alarmed. If this should happen, wait 30 minutes for the machine to cool, then push the black reset button on the bottom of the machine and resume normal use.

GETTING STARTED

As the Vita-Mix machine is different from ordinary kitchen appliances, it's best to try the no-fail recipes in this book before creating your own. Here are some general guidelines on some of the machine's most popular functions.

ONE MACHINE, MANY USES

The multi-functional Vita-Mix machine can perform numerous kitchen tasks, so that you are unlikely to ever need any other food appliance. It can:
• Juice whole fruits and vegetables to make whole-food juices and smoothies
• Create delicious ice creams, sorbets and other frozen desserts
• Cook steaming-hot soups from fresh raw produce
• Cream party-perfect spreads, dips & pâtés
• Make lump-free sauces and gravies
• Prepare salad dressings and marinades
• Whiz up all-natural fruit spreads, sauces and toppings
• Whip nutritious, creamy desserts
• Chop vegetables for stews and casseroles
• Shred vegetables for salads and coleslaws
• Chop cheese from coarse to fine
• Mince lean meats, preserving nutritional value and saving money
• Crumb bread quickly and easily
• Mill fresh and dried herbs
• Melt cheese or chocolate for quick and easy sauces and fondues
• Grind nuts and seeds to make fresh nut butters
• Mix batters for pancakes, crêpes and muffins
• Make non-dairy nut or soya-based milks
• Churn herb butters from fresh cream
• Frappé fabulous coffees
• Purée natural baby foods in a flash
• Crush ice

HOW TO MAKE WHOLE-FOOD JUICES AND SMOOTHIES

Unlike standard juicers, which extract the juice from fresh produce and lose as much as 70 per cent of the nutritional benefit (and money spent) in the 'waste' portion, the Vita-Mix machine results in almost no waste. Whole-food juices are made by blending fruits and/or vegetables with up to 30 per cent water, extracted juices or other liquids, and ice (to keep the drink cool).

Whole-food juices are the perfect raw food breakfast or snack. Because whole fruits and vegetables are completely pulverized when making juices in the Vita-Mix machine, you can toss in your favourite varieties – stems, seeds, pits and all – and process on HIGH for about 1 minute. Melon seeds, for example, can be added for extra fibre, pineapple cores can be incorporated for their anti-inflammatory properties and even small amounts of orange or lemon peel can be included for extra flavour and antioxidants. The Vita-Mix machine pulverizes them perfectly, delivering a creamy, smooth juice that is full of fibre, but with no fibre 'feel'.

1 Put the container on the motor base.

2 Put the soft foods in the container first, followed by liquids, then solid items. Add ice last.

3 Secure the 2-part lid. Select VARIABLE speed 1. Turn the machine on and quickly increase the speed to 10, then to HIGH. Blend until the desired consistency is achieved, using the tamper to push the ingredients into the blades if necessary.

Note: Drinks are best consumed straight away as this is when their nutritional value is at its greatest, and drinks tend to thicken if stored in the fridge.

HOW TO COOK WITH THE VITA-MIX MACHINE

The Vita-Mix machine uses friction heat generated by the high-speed rotation of the blades to cook food. This prevents valuable enzymes and nutrients in fresh fruit and vegetables being destroyed. Depending on thickness, soups cook in 4–8 minutes in the machine. Most vegetables can be added raw; however, potatoes, sweet potatoes, pumpkin, winter squash, pulses, beans and grains must be cooked before being processed in the Vita-Mix machine.

1 Put the container on the motor base.

2 Put the soft foods and liquids in the container first, solid items last.

3 Secure the 2-part lid. Select VARIABLE speed 1. Turn the machine on and quickly increase the speed to 10, then to HIGH. Run the machine until the desired temperature or consistency is achieved.

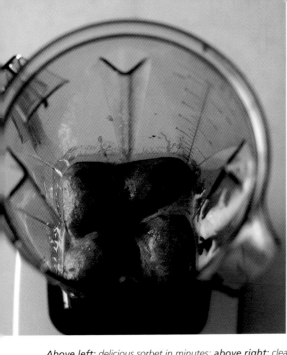

*Above left: delicious sorbet in minutes; **above right:** cleaning the tamper.*

HOW TO MAKE FROZEN MIXTURES

To make ice cream or sorbets, add frozen ingredients to the liquid, flavouring and sweetener. Blend it all together and you get a soft-serve frozen mixture. There are several important factors in making successful frozen desserts. Most importantly, make sure to use one part liquid to three to four parts frozen ingredients otherwise the mixture won't freeze stiffly enough.

1 Put the container on the motor base.

2 Put the liquids and soft foods in the container first. Next add sweeteners. Always add frozen ingredients last.

3 Lock the lid and insert the tamper through the lid plug opening.

4 Select VARIABLE speed 1. Turn the machine on and quickly increase the speed to 10, then to HIGH. Run the machine until the desired consistency is achieved, using the tamper to push the frozen ingredients into the blades to get the mixture flowing and blending quickly. Do not over-process as this may result in melting.

Note: If the mixture is too soft, like a milkshake, add more frozen ingredients through the lid plug opening and continue to blend. If you would like pieces of chopped fruit, chocolate or nuts in the finished ice cream, add them during the last few seconds of blending.

HOW TO CHOP FOOD

There are three ways in which you can chop food in the Vita-Mix machine: without water (dry chopping), with water (wet chopping) and pulsing.

DRY CHOPPING

The non-water method is best for small quantities of food or to chop soft food that shouldn't come in contact with water. It can, however, also be used for chopping larger quantities as long as this is done in batches.

Chopping is normally done on the VARIABLE speed dial: lower VARIABLE speeds produce a courser texture, and higher VARIABLE speeds produce smaller particles and a smoother texture. If the food bounces around on top of the blades without being chopped, you should increase the speed. If the food is violently thrown to the container walls and the particles are unevenly chopped, you should reduce the speed.

1 Put the container on the motor base.
2 Put small quantities of food in the container, working in batches if necessary.
3 Secure the 2-part lid. Select the desired VARIABLE speed and turn the machine on. Alternatively, the food can be dropped through the lid plug opening while the machine is running.

WET CHOPPING

To quickly chop or grind larger quantities of food, such as cabbage for coleslaw, potatoes for hash browns or even ice for crushing, use water to help circulate food through the blades. Be careful not to over-process.

1 Put the food in the container and cover it with cold water.
2 Put the container on the motor base.
3 Secure the 2-part lid. Select VARIABLE speed 5 and turn the machine on for about 5–10 seconds. If the food doesn't circulate, remove the lid plug and use the tamper to push it into the blades.
4 Pour into a strainer and drain well. Press out as much water as possible.

PULSING

Pulsing the Vita-Mix machine on and off is an effective way to chop small quantities of food or to chop soft foods (such as avocado) when a chunky consistency is required. Pulsing can also be used to coarsely chop herbs.

1 Put the container on the motor base.
2 Put the food in the container.
3 Secure the 2-part lid. Select VARIABLE or HIGH speed and pulse the machine on and off several times until the desired consistency is achieved.

Note: Due to varying ice temperatures, ice shapes and softness of food, the blending times may vary slightly from those mentioned in the recipes.

HOW TO USE THIS COOKBOOK

The 200 recipes in this book provide a wide range of choices for all tastes and preferences. To help you make the most of your Vita-Mix machine, the recipes have been divided into eight chapters – drinks, breakfasts, lunches, snacks and side dishes, dinners, desserts, special occasions, and babies and toddlers. This way you can prepare delicious drinks, snacks and meals any time for the whole family. Mix and match recipes from the different chapters or use them to plan your menus ahead of schedule for the entire week.

Many of the recipes are suitable for particular diets, so whether you are vegetarian, vegan, diabetic or have a food allergy or intolerance to dairy, eggs, wheat, gluten, nuts, seeds, citrus fruit or sugar, you will find a range of recipes to suit your needs. See page 20 for an overview of the easy-to-read symbols that accompany each recipe.

Even if a recipe doesn't fulfil your dietary criteria, many of the recipes include suggestions on how you can alter them to make them suitable – for example milk, yogurt and cream in drinks, smoothies, ice creams and sauces

can often easily be substituted with dairy-free alternatives, and recipes containing wheat or gluten can be modified to make them suitable for a wheat- or gluten-free diet.

On top of this, each recipe has a list of health benefits, so that you'll know at a glance whether it's energizing, detoxifying, immune-boosting, anti-ageing, stress-busting, weight-shifting, high protein, high fibre, low carb, low cholesterol, low saturated fat, low calorie or low kilojoule. See page 18 for an overview of these health benefits.

Unless stated, the majority of recipes can be made in either the 2-litre container or the smaller 32-ounce container without altering the quantities used. Some recipes will need to be halved if being made in the smaller container – where this is the case, the recipes have been clearly marked. Only a few recipes are not suitable for the 32-ounce container, and these are clearly indicated at the top of each recipe.

Enjoy the recipes in this book – they are simple, delicious and nourishing. Once you have prepared them you'll know how to make frozen treats, restaurant-quality smoothies, dips, hot soups and nutritious juices. Follow the directions carefully, and you'll quickly learn what the Vita-Mix machine can do. Soon you'll be developing delicious recipes of your own.

TIPS & CUSTOMER SERVICE

The Vita-Mix customer service team is always ready to assist you with any queries or technical questions you may have. We want to make sure that you are getting the most out of your Vita-Mix machine, so don't hesitate to contact us by post, email or via the Vita-Mix website (www.vitamix.co.uk) if you have any questions or require assistance.

TIPS

- Prefer a thinner juice? Just add a little water and run the Vita-Mix machine for a few seconds until the desired consistency is achieved.

- Prefer a firmer ice cream? Simply add additional frozen fruit or ice cubes to the mixture and run the machine for several seconds, but never longer than 1 minute.

- For smoother ice cream, use the tamper to press the mixture into the blades and run for a few seconds until the desired consistency is achieved.

- Machine stopped suddenly? The Vita-Mix machine automatically switches off to protect it from overheating. If this happens, wait 30 minutes for the machine to cool, then push the black reset button on the bottom of the machine and resume normal use.

Can't find the answer you need? Phone us!
The friendly and helpful Vita-Mix customer service team is always available to assist you with queries or technical help.

POST:
Vita-Mix Europe Ltd
The Old Library
6 Linden Rd
Clevedon
North Somerset
BS21 7SN
United Kingdom

EMAIL: service@vitamix.com

PHONE:
UK Local Rate: 08458 684 566
IE Local Rate: 0766 709 854
US Direct: +1 440 235 4840

INTERNET:
www.vitamix.co.uk
www.vitamix.ie

HEALTH BENEFITS

Eating for optimal nutrition is made easy with the Vita-Mix machine. The recipes in this book are designed to maximize the health benefits of the food you eat, and to help you to make the most of your Vita-Mix machine. Each recipe is made with wholesome, fresh ingredients. See each recipe to find out which of the following important health benefits apply.

ENERGIZING

Contains complex carbohydrates and/or various vitamins, minerals and other nutrients that may promote energy production in the body.

DETOXIFYING

Contains dietary fibre that helps cleanse the colon and/or vitamins, minerals, antioxidants and other nutrients that assist the body's detoxification process.

IMMUNE-BOOSTING

Contains vitamins, minerals, phytochemicals and other nutrients that support immune function.

ANTI-AGEING

Rich in antioxidants that may help reduce free radical damage and help slow down the ageing process.

STRESS-BUSTING

Contains nutrients such as B vitamins, vitamin C and magnesium that play an important role in strengthening the nervous system and supporting adrenal gland function.

WEIGHT-SHIFTING

Relatively low in calories or a good source of protein, healthy fats or fibre that aids satiety, which may promote weight loss in conjunction with an overall healthy eating plan.

HIGH PROTEIN

Contains foods high in protein, such as meat, poultry, fish, shellfish, dairy produce, eggs, tofu, nuts, seeds, beans and pulses.

HIGH FIBRE

Contains foods high in fibre, such as whole grains, beans, pulses, seeds, nuts, fruit and vegetables.

LOW CARB

Low in carbohydrate-containing foods, such as grains, fruit and sugar.

LOW CHOLESTEROL

Low in cholesterol-containing foods, such as meat, poultry, prawns, eggs, whole milk and other full-fat dairy products.

LOW SATURATED FAT

Low in foods that contain saturated fats, such as meat, poultry, eggs, whole milk and other full-fat dairy products, some margarines and coconut.

LOW CALORIE and LOW KILOJOULE

Low in calories/kilojoules and may aid weight loss in conjunction with an overall healthy eating plan.

Salsa

SERVES 4 **PREPARATION TIME:** 5 minutes **VITA-MIX TIME:** 10 seconds
SERVE WITH: Baked tortilla crisps **STORAGE:** This can be kept in the fridge for up to 1 day.

3 spring onions • ½ red chilli, deseeded • 4 coriander sprigs • 2 tomatoes, halved and deseeded
• juice and zest of 1 lime • 1 tsp sugar

1 Put the spring onions, chilli and coriander in the Vita-Mix machine, secure the 2-part lid and select
VARIABLE speed 1. Pulse on and off for 4–5 seconds until coarsely chopped. Transfer to a bowl.
2 Put the tomatoes into the Vita-Mix and secure the 2-part lid. Select VARIABLE speed 1 and pulse
on and off for 4–5 seconds until coarsely chopped. Add to the bowl, mix well and serve.

HEALTH BENEFITS • Immune-boosting • Weight-shifting • High fibre • Low carb • Low cholesterol
• Low saturated fat • Low calorie • Low kilojoule

Thai Curry Paste

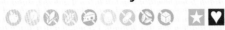

SERVES 4 **PREPARATION TIME:** 5 minutes **VITA-MIX TIME:** 21 seconds
USE IN: Curries and lentil dishes or add to soups, tagines and cooked rice, quinoa or beans.
STORAGE: This can be kept in the fridge for up to 1 week.

1 green chilli, deseeded • 1 shallot, halved • 1cm/½in piece root ginger, peeled • 2 dried kaffir lime
leaves • 1 lemongrass stalk • ½ tsp ground cumin • ½ tsp ground coriander • ½ tsp salt • 1 handful
coriander leaves • 4 tbsp olive oil • 1 tbsp lime juice

1 Put all the ingredients for the paste in the Vita-Mix machine and secure 2-part lid. Select VARIABLE speed
1. Turn the machine on and run for 6 seconds until combined. Stop the machine and scrape down the
mixture from the sides of the container, using a spatula.
2 Secure 2-part lid and select VARIABLE speed 1. Turn the machine on and increase the speed to 10, then
to HIGH. Run for a further 10–15 seconds until the mixture forms a paste.

HEALTH BENEFITS • Detoxifying • Immune-boosting • Weight-shifting • Low carb • Low cholesterol
• Low saturated fat • Low calorie • Low kilojoule

Mashed Potatoes

SERVES 4 **PREPARATION TIME:** 5 minutes **VITA-MIX TIME:** 7 seconds **COOKING TIME:** 17 minutes
SERVE WITH: Steak or grilled tofu **STORAGE:** Serve immediately.

1kg/2lb 3oz floury potatoes, peeled and cut into chunks • 200ml/7fl oz full-fat milk
• 30g/1oz butter or 1 tbsp olive oil

1 Bring a large pan of salted water to the boil over a high heat. Add the potatoes, then reduce the heat
to medium and simmer for 15 minutes or until tender. Drain well.
2 Put the milk in a saucepan and heat it over a medium heat for 2 minutes or until hot. Transfer to the
Vita-Mix machine and add the butter and potatoes. Secure the 2-part lid and select VARIABLE speed 1.
Turn the machine on and increase the speed to 6. Run for 6–7 seconds until the mixture forms a smooth
mash, using the tamper to push the potatoes into the blades. Serve immediately.

HEALTH BENEFITS • Energizing

Make this: dairy-free by using soya milk instead of full-fat milk.

Chocolate Sauce

MAKES: About 150ml/5fl oz **PREPARATION TIME:** 2 minutes **VITA-MIX TIME:** 4 minutes
COOKING TIME: 2 minutes **SERVE WITH:** Fruit **STORAGE:** This will keep in the fridge for up to 2 days.

125ml/4fl oz double cream • 50g/2oz butter •100g/3½oz light soft brown sugar • 50g/2oz dark chocolate

1 Heat the cream in a saucepan over a low heat for 2 minutes, stirring, until hot.
2 Put the cream and the remaining ingredients for the sauce in the Vita-Mix machine and secure the 2-part lid. Select VARIABLE speed 1. Turn the machine on and increase the speed to 10, then to HIGH. Run for 3–4 minutes until hot and thick, then serve.

HEALTH BENEFITS • Energizing • High protein

Fresh Fruit Sauce

MAKES: About 300ml/10½fl oz **PREPARATION TIME:** 3 minutes **VITA-MIX TIME:** 20 seconds
SERVE WITH: Yogurt or ice cream **STORAGE:** This will keep in the fridge for up to 3 days.

300g/10½oz strawberries or raspberries • 1 tbsp lime juice • 1–2 tbsp sugar

1 Put the strawberries, lime juice and sugar in the Vita-Mix machine and secure the 2-part lid. Select VARIABLE speed 1. Turn the machine on and quickly increase the speed to 10, then to HIGH.
2 Run for 20 seconds or until smooth, then serve.

HEALTH BENEFITS • Energizing • Detoxifying • Immune-boosting • Anti-ageing • Stress-busting
• Weight-shifting • High fibre • Low cholesterol • Low saturated fat • Low calorie • Low kilojoule

Basic Sweet Crumble Mixture

SERVES 4 **PREPARATION TIME:** 4 minutes **VITA-MIX TIME:** 8 seconds
SERVE WITH: Fruit or yogurt or use to make fruit crumbles
STORAGE: This can be kept in the fridge for up to 4 days.

140g/5oz rolled oats • 25g/1oz plain flour • 2 tbsp demerara sugar • a pinch of cinnamon
• 50g/1¾oz unsalted butter

1 Put the oats, flour, sugar and cinnamon in the Vita-Mix machine and secure the 2-part lid. Select VARIABLE speed 1. Turn the machine on and run for 6–8 seconds or until well mixed.
2 Transfer the mixture to a bowl and rub in the butter, using your fingertips, until the mixture forms a coarse crumble, then serve.

HEALTH BENEFITS • Energizing

Make this: *dairy-free by using vegetable margarine instead of butter.*

Drinks

Morning Glory Breakfast Smoothie

Apple Blush

SERVES 2 **PREPARATION TIME:** 5 minutes **VITA-MIX TIME:** 30 seconds
STORAGE: Best drunk straight away.

1 apple, quartered • 250g/9oz red seedless grapes • 250g/9oz strawberries • 300ml/10½fl oz apple juice • 8 ice cubes

1 Put the ingredients in the Vita-Mix machine in the order listed and secure the 2-part lid.
2 Select VARIABLE speed 1. Turn the machine on and increase the speed to 10, then to HIGH. Run for 30 seconds or until smooth. Pour into glasses and serve.

HEALTH BENEFITS • Energizing • Detoxifying • Immune-boosting • Anti-ageing • Stress-busting • Weight-shifting • High fibre • Low cholesterol • Low saturated fat • Low calorie • Low kilojoule

Carrot, Orange & Cantaloupe Medley

SERVES 2 **PREPARATION TIME:** 10 minutes **VITA-MIX TIME:** 30 seconds
STORAGE: Best drunk straight away.

1 large carrot, quartered • 1 orange, peeled and halved • ½ cantaloupe melon, peeled and deseeded (if desired) • 100ml/3½fl oz pineapple juice • 5mm/¼in piece root ginger, peeled (optional) • 6 ice cubes

1 Put the ingredients in the Vita-Mix machine in the order listed and secure the 2-part lid.
2 Select VARIABLE speed 1. Turn the machine on and increase the speed to 10, then to HIGH. Run for 30 seconds or until smooth, using the tamper to push the fruit into the blades. Pour into glasses and serve.

HEALTH BENEFITS • Energizing • Detoxifying • Immune-boosting • Anti-ageing • Stress-busting • Weight-shifting • High fibre • Low cholesterol • Low saturated fat • Low calorie • Low kilojoule

Watermelon Refresher

SERVES 2 **PREPARATION TIME:** 5 minutes **VITA-MIX TIME:** 30 seconds
STORAGE: Best drunk straight away.
NOT SUITABLE FOR THE 32oz CONTAINER.

¼ watermelon, peeled, deseeded (if desired) and chopped • 1 pear, halved and cored • 200g/7oz frozen strawberries

1 Put the ingredients in the Vita-Mix machine in the order listed and secure the 2-part lid.
2 Select VARIABLE speed 1. Turn the machine on and increase the speed to 10, then to HIGH. Run for 30 seconds or until smooth, using the tamper to push the ingredients into the blades. Pour into glasses and serve.

HEALTH BENEFITS • Energizing • Detoxifying • Immune-boosting • Anti-ageing • Stress-busting • Weight-shifting • High fibre • Low cholesterol • Low saturated fat • Low calorie • Low kilojoule

Peach & Raspberry Twist

SERVES 2 **PREPARATION TIME:** 5 minutes **VITA-MIX TIME:** 1 minute
STORAGE: Best drunk straight away.

100g/3½oz raspberries • 1 small peach, pitted and chopped • ½ orange, peeled and strips of peel
reserved to serve • ½ banana, peeled • 300ml/10½fl oz orange juice • 8 ice cubes • 2 mint sprigs, to serve

1 Put all the ingredients, except the orange peel and mint leaves, in the Vita-Mix machine in the order listed
and secure the 2-part lid.
2 Select VARIABLE speed 1. Turn the machine on and increase the speed to 10, then to HIGH. Run for
1 minute or until smooth. Pour into glasses and serve decorated with the orange peel and mint sprigs.

HEALTH BENEFITS • Energizing • Detoxifying • Immune-boosting • Anti-ageing • Stress-busting
• Weight-shifting • High fibre • Low cholesterol • Low saturated fat • Low calorie • Low kilojoule

Kiwi Cooler

SERVES 2 **PREPARATION TIME:** 5 minutes **VITA-MIX TIME:** 30 seconds
STORAGE: Best drunk straight away.

2 kiwi fruit, peeled and halved • 200g/7oz white seedless grapes • ½ banana, peeled
• ½ cucumber, peeled • 200ml/7fl oz apple juice • 8 ice cubes

1 Put the ingredients in the Vita-Mix machine in the order listed and secure the 2-part lid. Select VARIABLE speed 1. Turn the machine on and increase the speed to 10, then to HIGH.
2 Run for 30 seconds or until smooth. Pour into glasses and serve.

HEALTH BENEFITS • Energizing • Detoxifying • Immune-boosting • Anti-ageing • Stress-busting
• Weight-shifting • High fibre • Low cholesterol • Low saturated fat • Low calorie • Low kilojoule

Taste of the Tropics

SERVES 2 **PREPARATION TIME:** 10 minutes **VITA-MIX TIME:** 1 minute
STORAGE: Best drunk straight away.

⅓ pineapple, peeled and cut into chunks • ½ papaya, peeled and deseeded • ½ banana, peeled
• ¼ orange, peeled • 200ml/7fl oz pineapple juice • 1 tbsp lime juice • 8 ice cubes

1 Put the ingredients in the Vita-Mix machine in the order listed and secure the 2-part lid. Select VARIABLE speed 1. Turn the machine on and increase the speed to 10, then to HIGH.
2 Run for 1 minute or until smooth. Pour into glasses and serve.

HEALTH BENEFITS • Energizing • Detoxifying • Immune-boosting • Anti-ageing • Stress-busting
• Weight-shifting • High fibre • Low cholesterol • Low saturated fat • Low calorie • Low kilojoule

Bitter Melon

SERVES 2 **PREPARATION TIME:** 10 minutes **VITA-MIX TIME:** 30 seconds
STORAGE: Best drunk straight away.

½ honeydew or galia melon, peeled and deseeded (if desired) • 100g/3½oz white seedless grapes
• 1 tangerine, peeled • 1–2 grapefruit segments • 100ml/3½fl oz white grape juice • 8 ice cubes

1 Put the ingredients in the Vita-Mix machine in the order listed and secure the 2-part lid. Select VARIABLE speed 1. Turn the machine on and increase the speed to 10, then to HIGH.
2 Run for 30 seconds or until smooth. Pour into glasses and serve.

HEALTH BENEFITS • Energizing • Detoxifying • Immune-boosting • Anti-ageing • Stress-busting
• Weight-shifting • High fibre • Low cholesterol • Low saturated fat • Low calorie • Low kilojoule

Teriyaki Tomato Juice

SERVES 2 **PREPARATION TIME:** 5 minutes **VITA-MIX TIME:** 1 minute
STORAGE: Best drunk straight away.

1 celery stick, quartered • ¼ green pepper, deseeded • 1 carrot, halved • ¼ small onion
• 400ml/14fl oz tomato juice • 2 tbsp teriyaki sauce • 6 ice cubes

1 Put the ingredients in the Vita-Mix machine in the order listed and secure the 2-part lid.
2 Select VARIABLE speed 1. Turn the machine on and increase the speed to 10, then to HIGH.
   Run for 1 minute or until smooth. Pour into glasses and serve.

HEALTH BENEFITS • Energizing • Detoxifying • Immune-boosting • Anti-ageing • Stress-busting
• Weight-shifting • High fibre • Low carb • Low cholesterol • Low saturated fat • Low calorie
• Low kilojoule

Digest Aid

SERVES 2 **PREPARATION TIME:** 5 minutes **VITA-MIX TIME:** 1 minute
STORAGE: Best drunk straight away.

½ pineapple, peeled and cut into chunks • ½ papaya, peeled and deseeded • 200ml/7fl oz pineapple
juice • 1cm/½in root ginger, peeled (if desired) • 1 tbsp clear honey • 8 ice cubes

1 Put the ingredients in the Vita-Mix machine in the order listed and secure the 2-part lid. Select VARIABLE
   speed 1. Turn the machine on and increase the speed to 10, then to HIGH.
2 Run for 1 minute or until smooth. Pour into glasses and serve.

HEALTH BENEFITS • Energizing • Detoxifying • Immune-boosting • Anti-ageing • Stress-busting
• Weight-shifting • High fibre • Low cholesterol • Low saturated fat • Low calorie • Low kilojoule

Make this: *sugar-free and vegan by omitting the honey.*

DRINKS

Triple Berry Surprise

SERVES 2 **PREPARATION TIME:** 5 minutes **VITA-MIX TIME:** 1 minute
STORAGE: Best drunk straight away.

200g/7oz strawberries • 200g/7oz blueberries • 100g/3½oz frozen raspberries
• 300ml/10½fl oz pomegranate juice • 8 ice cubes

1 Put the ingredients in the Vita-Mix machine in the order listed and secure the 2-part lid. Select VARIABLE
  speed 1. Turn the machine on and increase the speed to 10, then to HIGH.
2 Run for 1 minute or until smooth. Pour into glasses and serve.

HEALTH BENEFITS • Energizing • Detoxifying • Immune-boosting • Anti-ageing • Stress-busting
• Weight-shifting • High fibre • Low cholesterol • Low saturated fat • Low calorie • Low kilojoule

Californian Detox

SERVES 2 **PREPARATION TIME:** 10 minutes **VITA-MIX TIME:** 1 minute
STORAGE: Best drunk straight away.

2 carrots, quartered • 2 celery sticks, quartered • 1 small beetroot, halved • ½ fennel bulb
• ½ apple, cored (if desired) • 3 flat-leaf parsley sprigs • 8 ice cubes

1 Put the ingredients in the Vita-Mix machine in the order listed, adding 400ml/14fl oz water before
putting the ice cubes in. Secure the 2-part lid and select VARIABLE speed 1.
2 Turn the machine on and increase the speed to 10, then to HIGH. Run for 1 minute or until smooth,
using the tamper to push the vegetables into the blades. Pour into glasses and serve.

HEALTH BENEFITS • Energizing • Detoxifying • Immune-boosting • Anti-ageing • Stress-busting
• Weight-shifting • High fibre • Low cholesterol • Low saturated fat • Low calorie • Low kilojoule

Mango Delight

SERVES 2 **PREPARATION TIME:** 5 minutes **VITA-MIX TIME:** 1 minute
STORAGE: Best drunk straight away.

1 mango, peeled and chopped • ½ apple • 1 nectarine, halved and pitted • 250ml/9fl oz apple juice
• 8 ice cubes

1 Put the ingredients in the Vita-Mix machine in the order listed and secure the 2-part lid.
2 Select VARIABLE speed 1. Turn the machine on and increase the speed to 10, then to HIGH. Run for
1 minute or until smooth, using the tamper to push the fruit into the blades. Pour into glasses and serve.

HEALTH BENEFITS • Energizing • Detoxifying • Immune-boosting • Anti-ageing • Stress-busting
• Weight-shifting • High fibre • Low cholesterol • Low saturated fat • Low calorie • Low kilojoule

DRINKS

34

Grapefruit Combo

SERVES 2 **PREPARATION TIME:** 5 minutes **VITA-MIX TIME:** 30 seconds
STORAGE: Best drunk straight away.

½ red grapefruit, peeled • ½ orange, peeled • 200g/7oz white seedless grapes
• 200ml/7fl oz orange juice • ¼ banana, peeled (optional) • 8 ice cubes

1 Put the ingredients in the Vita-Mix machine in the order listed and secure the 2-part lid.
2 Select VARIABLE speed 1. Turn the machine on and increase the speed to 10, then to HIGH.
Run for 30 seconds or until smooth. Pour into glasses and serve.

HEALTH BENEFITS • Energizing • Detoxifying • Immune-boosting • Anti-ageing • Stress-busting
• Weight-shifting • High fibre • Low cholesterol • Low saturated fat • Low calorie • Low kilojoule

Blueberry Kiss

SERVES 2 **PREPARATION TIME:** 5 minutes, plus 4–5 hours for freezing the banana
VITA-MIX TIME: 30 seconds **STORAGE:** Best drunk straight away.

150g/5½oz blueberries • 300ml/10½fl oz semi-skimmed milk • 200ml/7fl oz natural yogurt
• ¼ tsp vanilla extract • 1 banana, peeled, chopped and frozen

1 Put the ingredients in the Vita-Mix machine in the order listed and secure the 2-part lid.
2 Select VARIABLE speed 1. Turn the machine on and increase the speed to 10, then to HIGH.
Run for 30 seconds or until smooth. Pour into glasses and serve.

HEALTH BENEFITS • Energizing • Immune-boosting • Anti-ageing • Stress-busting • Weight-shifting
• High protein • High fibre • Low cholesterol • Low saturated fat • Low calorie • Low kilojoule

Make this: vegan and dairy-free by using soya milk and yogurt instead of semi-skimmed milk
and natural yogurt.

Chocolate–Mint Soya Shake

SERVES 2 **PREPARATION TIME:** 5 minutes **VITA-MIX TIME:** 25 seconds
STORAGE: Best drunk straight away.

500ml/17fl oz sweetened soya milk • 250ml/9fl oz vanilla soya ice cream • 4 pitted dates
• 2 tbsp cocoa powder • 25g/1oz dark chocolate • 10 mint leaves • 1 tsp vanilla extract

1 Put the ingredients in the Vita-Mix machine in the order listed and secure the 2-part lid.
2 Select VARIABLE speed 1. Turn the machine on and run for 5 seconds, then increase the speed
to 10, and then to HIGH. Run for 20 seconds or until smooth. Pour into glasses and serve.

HEALTH BENEFITS • Energizing • High protein • Low cholesterol • Low saturated fat

DRINKS

Choco Monkey Smoothie

SERVES 2 **PREPARATION TIME:** 5 minutes, plus 4–5 hours for freezing the banana
VITA-MIX TIME: 30 seconds **STORAGE:** Best drunk straight away.

420ml/14½fl oz full-fat milk • 1 tbsp cocoa powder • 1–2 tbsp peanut butter • ½ tsp vanilla extract
• 1 large banana, peeled, chopped and frozen

1 Put the ingredients in the Vita-Mix machine in the order listed and secure the 2-part lid.
2 Select VARIABLE speed 1. Turn the machine on and increase the speed to 10, then to HIGH.
Run for 30 seconds or until smooth. Pour into glasses and serve.

HEALTH BENEFITS • Energizing • Stress-busting • High protein • High fibre

Make this: vegan and dairy-free by using soya or nut milk instead of full-fat milk.

Pineapple Passion Cup

SERVES 2 **PREPARATION TIME:** 10 minutes **VITA-MIX TIME:** 25 seconds
STORAGE: Best drunk straight away.

4 passionfruit • ½ pineapple, peeled, cored (if desired) and cut into chunks • 150ml/5fl oz coconut water
• 150ml/5fl oz coconut milk • 8 ice cubes

1 Cut the passionfruit in half and scoop the seeds into a fine sieve set over a bowl. Using the back
of a teaspoon, press the pulp through. Discard the seeds.
2 Put the passionfruit juice in the Vita-Mix machine and add the remaining ingredients in the order listed.
Secure the 2-part lid and select VARIABLE speed 1. Turn the machine on and increase the speed to 10,
then to HIGH. Run for 25 seconds or until smooth. Pour into glasses and serve.

HEALTH BENEFITS • Energizing • Detoxifying • Immune-boosting • Anti-ageing • Stress-busting
• Weight-shifting • High fibre • Low cholesterol • Low saturated fat • Low calorie • Low kilojoule

Mango & Cashew Lassi

SERVES 2 **PREPARATION TIME:** 10 minutes **VITA-MIX TIME:** 30 seconds
STORAGE: Best drunk straight away.

500ml/17fl oz natural yogurt • 200ml/7fl oz full-fat milk • 2 mangoes, peeled and chopped • 2 tsp sugar
• 55g/2oz cashew nuts • 4 cardamom pods • 8 ice cubes

1 Put the ingredients in the Vita-Mix machine in the order listed and secure the 2-part lid.
2 Select VARIABLE speed 1. Turn the machine on and increase the speed to 10, then to HIGH.
   Run for 30 seconds or until smooth. Pour into glasses and serve.

HEALTH BENEFITS • Energizing • Immune-boosting • Anti-ageing • Stress-busting • High protein
• High fibre

Make this: *vegan and dairy-free by using soya milk and yogurt instead of full-fat milk and natural
yogurt. Make this nut-free by omitting the cashew nuts.*

Morning Glory Breakfast Smoothie

SERVES 2 **PREPARATION TIME:** 10 minutes, plus 4–5 hours for freezing the banana
VITA-MIX TIME: 30 seconds **STORAGE:** Best drunk straight away.

¼ orange, peeled • 250ml/9fl oz natural yogurt • 300ml/10½fl oz pomegranate juice
• 125g/4½oz frozen blueberries • ½ banana, peeled, chopped and frozen • ½ tsp bee pollen
granules (optional) • ½ tsp shelled hemp seeds (optional) • ½ tsp lecithin granules (optional)

1 Put the ingredients in the Vita-Mix machine in the order listed and secure the 2-part lid.
2 Select VARIABLE speed 1. Turn the machine on and increase the speed to 10, then to HIGH.
   Run for 30 seconds or until smooth. Pour into glasses and serve.

HEALTH BENEFITS • Energizing • Detoxifying • Immune-boosting • Anti-ageing • Stress-busting
• Weight-shifting • High fibre • Low cholesterol • Low saturated fat • Low calorie • Low kilojoule

Make this: *vegan and dairy-free by using soya yogurt instead of natural yogurt and omitting the pollen.*

Goji Almond Whiz

SERVES 2 **PREPARATION TIME:** 5 minutes **VITA-MIX TIME:** 1 minute
STORAGE: Best drunk straight away.

500ml/17fl oz rice milk • 20g/¾oz almonds • 20g/¾oz dried goji berries • 100g/3½oz raspberries
• ½ banana, peeled • 4 tsp clear honey • 8 ice cubes

1 Put the ingredients in the Vita-Mix machine in the order listed and secure the 2-part lid.
2 Select VARIABLE speed 1. Turn the machine on and increase the speed to 10, then to HIGH.
Run for 1 minute or until smooth. Pour into glasses and serve.

HEALTH BENEFITS • Energizing • Immune-boosting • Anti-ageing • Stress-busting • Weight-shifting
• High fibre • Low cholesterol • Low saturated fat

Make this: *vegan by using agave syrup instead of honey.*

Spiced Hot Chocolate

SERVES 2 **PREPARATION TIME:** 10 minutes **VITA-MIX TIME:** 6 minutes
STORAGE: Best drunk straight away.

600ml/21fl oz full-fat milk • 100ml/3½fl oz single cream (optional) • 1 tbsp cocoa powder
• 1 tbsp sugar • ½ vanilla pod, split and seeds scraped out OR ½ tsp vanilla extract
• a pinch cinnamon • 100ml/3½fl oz double cream, whipped • 30g/1oz dark chocolate, grated
• a pinch nutmeg

1 Put the milk, single cream, cocoa powder, sugar, vanilla and cinnamon in the Vita-Mix machine
in the order listed. Secure the 2-part lid and select VARIABLE speed 1. Turn the machine on and increase
the speed to 10, then to HIGH. Run for 6 minutes or until hot.
2 Pour the hot chocolate into mugs and top with the whipped cream. Sprinkle with the grated chocolate
and nutmeg and serve immediately.

HEALTH BENEFITS • Energizing • Stress-busting • High protein • Low carb

Make this: vegan and dairy-free by using soya milk and cream instead of full-fat milk and cream.
Make this lower in calories by using skimmed milk and omitting the cream.

Almond or Cashew Milk

SERVES 2 **PREPARATION TIME:** 3 minutes **VITA-MIX TIME:** 1 minute
STORAGE: Best drunk straight away.

200g/7oz almonds or cashew nuts • 1 tsp sugar • ¼ tsp vanilla extract (optional)

1 Put the almonds or cashew nuts in the Vita-Mix machine with 600ml/21fl oz water.
2 Add the sugar and vanilla extract, if using, and secure the 2-part lid. Select VARIABLE speed 1. Turn the machine on and increase the speed to 10, then to HIGH. Run for 1 minute or until smooth, and serve.

HEALTH BENEFITS • Energizing • Detoxifying • Immune-boosting • Anti-ageing • Stress-busting • Weight-shifting • High protein • High fibre • Low carb • Low cholesterol • Low saturated fat

Make this: *sugar-free by omitting the sugar.*

Raspberry Mojito

SERVES 2 **PREPARATION TIME:** 5 minutes **VITA-MIX TIME:** 15 seconds
STORAGE: Best drunk straight away.

12 raspberries • 4½ tsp brown sugar • juice of 2 limes • 125ml/4fl oz rum
• 1 tbsp grenadine • 4 ice cubes • 1 large handful mint leaves • 2–3 tbsp soda water

1 Put the raspberries, sugar and lime juice in the Vita-Mix machine, secure the 2-part lid and select VARIABLE speed 1. Turn the machine on and increase the speed to 5. Run for 10 seconds.
2 Reduce the speed to 1, remove the lid plug and slowly pour in the rum and grenadine and run for a further 2–3 seconds until combined. Turn the machine off.
3 Add the ice cubes and mint, and replace the lid plug. Select HIGH and pulse on and off a few times to crush the ice lightly. Pour into cocktail glasses, top with the soda water to taste and serve.

HEALTH BENEFITS • Low cholesterol • Low saturated fat

Asian Passion

SERVES 2 **PREPARATION TIME:** 5 minutes **VITA-MIX TIME:** 13 seconds
STORAGE: Best drunk straight away.

2 passionfruit • 2 tsp brandy • 1 tsp caster sugar • ½ peach, pitted, plus 2 slices, to serve
• 230ml/7¾fl oz champagne

1 Cut the passionfruit in half and scoop the seeds into a fine sieve set over a bowl. Using the back
   of a teaspoon, press the pulp through. Discard the seeds.
2 Put the passionfruit juice, brandy, sugar and peach in the Vita-Mix machine and secure the 2-part lid.
   Select VARIABLE speed 1. Turn the machine on and increase the speed to 6. Run for 10 seconds or until
   smooth, using the tamper to push the fruit into the blades if necessary. Turn the machine off.
3 Add the champagne. Select VARIABLE speed 2 and run the machine for 2–3 seconds. Pour into
   cocktail glasses, decorate each one with 1 slice of peach and serve.

HEALTH BENEFITS • Low cholesterol • Low saturated fat

Mai Tai

SERVES 2 **PREPARATION TIME:** 5 minutes **VITA-MIX TIME:** 15 seconds

40ml/1¼fl oz white rum • 40ml/1¼fl oz apricot brandy • 40ml/1¼fl oz triple sec • juice of 1 lime
• 230ml/7¾fl oz pineapple juice • 2 tbsp orange juice • 6 ice cubes

1 Put all the ingredients, except the ice cubes, in the Vita-Mix machine and secure the 2-part lid.
   Select VARIABLE speed 3 and run for 10 seconds.
2 Remove the lid plug and add the ice, then replace the lid plug and select VARIABLE speed 6.
   Pulse on and off 3–4 times to crush the ice lightly. Pour into glasses and serve immediately.

HEALTH BENEFITS • Low cholesterol • Low saturated fat

Lycheetini

SERVES 2 **PREPARATION TIME:** 5 minutes **VITA-MIX TIME:** 13 seconds
STORAGE: Best drunk straight away.

2 tbsp caster sugar • 150ml/5fl oz lychee juice • 80ml/2½fl oz gin • 80ml/2½fl oz vodka
• 2 lychees, peeled

1 Put the sugar, lychee juice and 4 tbsp water in the Vita-Mix machine and secure the 2-part lid.
   Select VARIABLE speed 1. Turn the machine on and increase the speed to 10, then to HIGH.
   Run for 10 seconds or until the sugar dissolves completely. Switch off the machine.
2 Add the gin and vodka and secure the 2-part lid. Select VARIABLE speed 3 and run for 2–3 seconds
   to combine. Pour into glasses and garnish each one with 1 lychee speared on a cocktail stick.

HEALTH BENEFITS • Low cholesterol • Low saturated fat

Strawberry Daiquiri

SERVES 2 **PREPARATION TIME:** 5 minutes **VITA-MIX TIME:** 12 seconds
STORAGE: Best drunk straight away.

85ml/2¾fl oz white rum • 4 tbsp strawberry liqueur • juice of 1 lime • 1 tbsp caster sugar
• 10 strawberries • 6 ice cubes

1 Put all the ingredients, except the ice cubes, in the Vita-Mix machine and secure the 2-part lid.
   Select VARIABLE speed 3 and run for 2–3 seconds, then increase the speed to 10, then to HIGH.
   Run for 5–6 seconds then switch off the machine.
2 Add the ice cubes. Select VARIABLE speed 3 and pulse on and off 3–4 times to crush the ice lightly.
   Pour into glasses and serve.

HEALTH BENEFITS • Low cholesterol • Low saturated fat

Breakfasts

Apple & Cranberry Muffins

Mango, Banana & Sharon Fruit Whip

SERVES 4 **PREPARATION TIME:** 10 minutes, plus 20 minutes chilling **VITA-MIX TIME:** 30 seconds
SERVE WITH: Desiccated coconut sprinkled on top **STORAGE:** This will keep in the fridge for
up to 2 days. **IF USING THE 32oz CONTAINER:** Halve the quantities.

500g/1lb 2oz firm tofu, diced • 300ml/10½fl oz apple juice • 5 tbsp sunflower oil • 2 tbsp clear honey
• 2 bananas, peeled and halved • 2 mangoes, peeled, pitted and chopped • 1 sharon fruit, halved

1 Put the tofu, apple juice, oil and honey in the Vita-Mix machine and secure the 2-part lid. Select
   VARIABLE speed 1. Turn the machine on and increase the speed to 10, then to HIGH. Run for
   20 seconds or until smooth and creamy.
2 Remove the lid plug and add the bananas, mangoes and sharon fruit. Replace the plug and run
   on VARIABLE speed 6 for 10 seconds, using the tamper to push the fruit into the blades if necessary.
   Spoon into bowls, cover and chill for 20 minutes, then serve.

HEALTH BENEFITS • Energizing • Immune-boosting • Anti-ageing • Stress-busting • Weight-shifting
• High protein • High fibre • Low cholesterol • Low saturated fat • Low calorie • Low kilojoule

Make this: *vegan by replacing the honey with brown rice syrup.*

Cashew & Apricot Millet Porridge

SERVES 4 **PREPARATION TIME:** 5 minutes **VITA-MIX TIME:** 10 seconds **COOKING TIME:** 30 minutes
STORAGE: Best served straight away, but can be kept in the fridge for up to 1 day. Reheat in a saucepan
with some extra milk and simmer, stirring, until warmed through.

135g/4¾oz millet • 270ml/9½fl oz skimmed milk • 50g/1¾oz cashew nuts • 70g/2½oz dried apricots
• 1 tsp cinnamon • 1 tbsp maple syrup • 1 tbsp sugar (optional) • 1 tsp vanilla extract

1 Put the millet and 750ml/26fl oz water in a saucepan and bring to the boil over a high heat. Reduce
   the heat and simmer, covered, for 30 minutes or until all the water has been absorbed. Set aside.
2 Put the remaining ingredients in the Vita-Mix machine and secure the 2-part lid. Select VARIABLE speed 1.
   Turn the machine on and increase the speed to 10, then to HIGH. Run for 10 seconds or until smooth.
3 Add the mixture to the millet and mix well. Serve hot or cold.

HEALTH BENEFITS • Energizing • Detoxifying • Immune-boosting • Anti-ageing • Stress-busting
• High protein • High fibre • Low cholesterol • Low saturated fat

Make this: *vegan and dairy-free by using soya milk instead of skimmed milk.*

Blueberry Yogurt Crunch

 ♥

SERVES 4 **PREPARATION TIME:** 5 minutes **VITA-MIX TIME:** 25 seconds **COOKING TIME:** 2–3 minutes
STORAGE: This will keep in the fridge for up to 2 days.

55g/2oz desiccated coconut • 500ml/17fl oz natural yogurt • 200g/7oz blueberries, plus extra to serve
• ½ banana, peeled • 1 tsp vanilla extract • 2 tbsp clear honey • 200g/7oz granola

1 Put the coconut in a heavy-based saucepan over a medium heat and cook, stirring continuously,
   for 2–3 minutes until lightly toasted.
2 Put the yogurt, blueberries, banana, vanilla, honey and toasted coconut in the Vita-Mix machine
   and secure the 2-part lid. Select VARIABLE speed 5 and run for 20 seconds until combined.
3 While the machine is With the machine still running, remove the lid plug and add the granola. Run for
   a further 5 seconds, being careful not to over-mix, so it stays crunchy. Serve topped with the extra berries.

HEALTH BENEFITS • Energizing • Immune-boosting • Anti-ageing • Stress-busting • High fibre
• Low cholesterol • Low saturated fat

Make this: *vegan and dairy-free by using soya yogurt instead of natural yogurt and by using agave
syrup or brown rice syrup instead of honey.*

Pear, Fig & Coconut Porridge

SERVES 4 **PREPARATION TIME:** 5 minutes **VITA-MIX TIME:** 2 minutes **COOKING TIME:** 3 minutes
STORAGE: Best served straight away, but can be kept in the fridge for up to 1 day. To reheat, put
in a saucepan with some extra milk and simmer, stirring, until warmed through.
IF USING THE 32oz CONTAINER: Halve the quantities.

1.25l/44fl oz skimmed milk • 185g/6½oz porridge oats • 2 pears, cored and chopped
• 6 ready-to-eat dried figs • 4 tbsp desiccated coconut • 2 tbsp brown sugar • 2 tsp mixed spice
• a pinch salt • 2 figs, cut into wedges, to serve

1 Put the milk in a saucepan and heat over a medium-low heat for 2–3 minutes or until warmed through.
2 Put the milk and oats in the Vita-Mix machine and secure the 2-part lid. Select VARIABLE speed 1. Turn
   the machine on and increase the speed to 6. Run for 1 minute.
3 While the machine is still running, add the remaining ingredients through the lid plug opening. Run for
   a further 1 minute, using the tamper to push the ingredients into the blades. Divide into four bowls, top
   with the extra figs and serve immediately.

HEALTH BENEFITS • Energizing • Detoxifying • Immune-boosting • Anti-ageing • Stress-busting
• Weight-shifting • High protein • High fibre • Low cholesterol • Low saturated fat • Low calorie
• Low kilojoule

Make this: *vegan and dairy-free by using soya milk instead of skimmed milk. Make this gluten-free
by using millet flakes instead of oats.*

Deluxe Bircher Muesli

SERVES 4 **PREPARATION TIME:** 10 minutes, plus 30 minutes soaking **VITA-MIX TIME:** 15 seconds
STORAGE: This will keep in the fridge for up to 1 day.
IF USING THE 32oz CONTAINER: Halve the quantities.

200ml/7fl oz semi-skimmed milk • 200ml/7fl oz natural yogurt • 1 apple, halved and cored
• 2 apricots, halved and pitted • 2 tbsp honey • 25g/1oz mixed nuts, such as hazelnuts, almonds
and Brazil nuts • 5 dried dates • 200g/7oz muesli base or porridge oats • 2 tbsp raisins or sultanas
• 1 tbsp dried blueberries • 1 tbsp dried cherries • 1 tbsp sunflower seeds

1 Put the milk, yogurt, apple, apricots and honey in the Vita-Mix machine and secure the 2-part lid. Select
  VARIABLE speed 5 and run for 10 seconds or until well mixed.
2 While the machine is still running, remove the lid plug and add the nuts, dates and muesli. Replace the lid
  plug and run for a further 5 seconds.
3 Transfer the muesli to a large bowl and stir in the raisins, blueberries, cherries and sunflower seeds. Leave
  to soak for 30 minutes, then serve.

HEALTH BENEFITS • Energizing • Immune-boosting • Anti-ageing • Stress-busting • High protein
• High fibre • Low cholesterol • Low saturated fat

Make this: *nut-free by using pumpkin seeds and extra sunflower seeds instead of nuts.*

Lemony Corn Muffins

MAKES 6–8 muffins **PREPARATION TIME:** 15 minutes **VITA-MIX TIME**: 20 seconds
COOKING TIME: 20–25 minutes **STORAGE:** Keep in an airtight container for up to 2 days or freeze
for up to 1 month.

5 tbsp sunflower oil, plus extra for greasing • 125g/4½ oz self-raising flour • 125g/4½oz maize meal
• 115g/4oz brown sugar • 1 tsp baking powder • ½ tsp bicarbonate of soda • a pinch salt • 2 eggs
• 170ml/5½fl oz full-fat milk • zest of 2 lemons • 2 tsp lemon extract

1 Preheat the oven to 190°C/375°F/Gas 5 and grease 6 or 8 holes of a muffin tin with oil. Put the flour,
  maize meal, sugar, baking powder, bicarbonate of soda and salt in the Vita-Mix machine and secure
  the 2-part lid. Select VARIABLE speed 5 and run for 10 seconds or until well mixed.
2 Remove the lid plug and add the oil, eggs, milk, lemon zest and extract. Replace the lid plug and run
  for a further 10 seconds or until thoroughly combined, using the tamper to push the ingredients into
  the blades if necessary.
3 Spoon the mixture into the muffin tin and bake for 20–25 minutes until well risen and golden brown.
  Remove from the oven and leave to cool for 5–10 minutes, then remove from the tin and transfer to
  a wire rack to cool completely before serving.

HEALTH BENEFITS • Energizing

Apple & Cranberry Muffins

MAKES 8–10 muffins **PREPARATION TIME:** 10 minutes **VITA-MIX TIME:** 25 seconds
COOKING TIME: 25 minutes **STORAGE:** Keep in an airtight container for up to 2 days or freeze
for up to 1 month.

100ml/3½fl oz sunflower oil, plus extra for greasing • 300g/10½oz plain flour • 100g/3½oz caster sugar
• 2 tsp baking powder • ½ tsp cinnamon • 2 eggs • 100ml/3½fl oz full-fat milk • 2 small eating apples,
quartered and cored • 1 tsp vanilla extract • 100g/3½oz dried cranberries

1 Preheat the oven to 190°C/375°F/Gas 5 and grease 8 or 10 holes of a muffin tin with oil. Put the flour,
sugar, baking powder and cinnamon in the Vita-Mix machine and secure the 2-part lid. Select VARIABLE
speed 5 and run for 10 seconds or until well mixed.
2 Remove the lid plug and add the oil, eggs, milk, apples and vanilla. Replace the lid plug and run for
a further 15 seconds or until thoroughly combined, using the tamper to push the ingredients into the
blades. Turn the Vita-Mix machine off and stir in the dried cranberries.
3 Spoon the mixture into the muffin tin and bake for 25 minutes until risen and golden brown. Remove
from the oven and leave to cool for 5–10 minutes, then remove from the tin and transfer to a wire rack
to cool completely before serving.

HEALTH BENEFITS • Energizing

Waffles with Raspberry Sauce

SERVES 4 **PREPARATION TIME:** 15 minutes **VITA-MIX TIME:** 40 seconds
COOKING TIME: 16 minutes **STORAGE:** Best served straight away, although the sauce can be made
in advance and kept in the fridge for up to 3 days.

Sauce 300g/10½oz raspberries • 2 tbsp caster sugar • 2 tbsp lemon juice
Waffles 200g/7oz plain flour • 1 tsp baking powder • 50g/1¾oz caster sugar • 1 egg
• 200ml/7fl oz buttermilk or natural yogurt • 1 tsp vanilla extract • vegetable oil, for greasing

1 Put all the ingredients for the sauce in the Vita-Mix machine and secure the 2-part lid. Select VARIABLE
speed 1. Turn the machine on and increase the speed to 10, then to HIGH. Run for 20 seconds or until
smooth. Transfer to a container and set aside. Wash the Vita-Mix machine.
2 Put the flour, baking powder, sugar, egg, buttermilk and vanilla in the Vita-Mix machine and secure the
2-part lid. Select VARIABLE speed 1. Turn the machine on and increase the speed to 10, then to HIGH.
Run for 20 seconds or until thoroughly combined.
3 Lightly grease a waffle iron with oil and heat until hot. Pour some of the waffle mixture into the iron
and cook for 3–4 minutes or until golden brown. Transfer to a plate and repeat with the remaining
batter to make 4 waffles. Serve immediately with the sauce.

HEALTH BENEFITS • Energizing

Buckwheat Blinis with Maple Syrup & Hazelnut Cream

SERVES 4 **PREPARATION TIME:** 10 minutes, plus 15 minutes resting **VITA-MIX TIME:** 50 seconds
COOKING TIME: 16 minutes **STORAGE:** The blinis are best served straight away; the hazelnut cream can be made in advance and kept in an airtight container in the fridge for up to 2 days.

Hazelnut cream 500g/1lb 2oz crème fraîche • 200g/7oz blanched hazelnuts • 1 tbsp caster sugar
• 1 tsp vanilla extract • a pinch nutmeg
Blinis 70g/2½oz buckwheat flour • 30g/1oz plain flour • 1 tsp baking powder • 1 tsp caster sugar
(optional) • 1 egg • 150ml/5fl oz full-fat milk • 2–3 tbsp vegetable oil • 4 tbsp maple syrup

1 Put all the ingredients for the hazelnut cream in the Vita-Mix machine and secure the 2-part lid. Select VARIABLE speed 1. Turn the machine on and increase the speed to 10, then to HIGH. Run for 30 seconds or until thoroughly combined. Transfer to a container and set aside. Wash the Vita-Mix machine.
2 Put the flours, baking powder, sugar, egg and milk in the Vita-Mix machine and secure the 2-part lid. Select VARIABLE speed 1. Turn the machine on and increase the speed to 6. Run for 20 seconds or until thoroughly combined. Leave to rest for 15 minutes.
3 Heat 1 tablespoon of the oil in a non-stick frying pan over a medium heat. Add 3 heaped tablespoons of the batter to the pan, spacing them well apart, to make 3 x 10cm/4in blinis. Cook for 1–2 minutes or until bubbles start to appear on the surface, then turn the blinis over and cook for a further 1–2 minutes. Transfer to a plate and repeat with the remaining batter to make 12 blinis, adding more oil to the pan as needed.
4 Top the blinis with the hazelnut cream, then drizzle with the maple syrup and serve.

HEALTH BENEFITS • Energizing • High protein

Eggs Benedict with Parma Ham

SERVES 4 **PREPARATION TIME:** 5 minutes **VITA-MIX TIME:** 5 minutes 35 seconds
COOKING TIME: 8 minutes **STORAGE:** The hollandaise sauce can be made in advance and kept in the fridge for up to 1 day. Reheat gently in a saucepan over a low heat or whip up again in the Vita-Mix machine for 2 minutes on HIGH.

Hollandaise sauce 250g/9oz butter • 4 egg yolks • 1 tsp white wine vinegar • 5–6 tarragon leaves • 1 tsp lemon juice • a pinch cayenne pepper • salt and freshly ground black pepper
Eggs Benedict 4 eggs • 2 English muffins, halved horizontally • 1 tsp butter • 4 slices of Parma ham

1 To make the sauce, melt the butter in a saucepan over a low heat and skim off any white solids from the surface. Keep warm. Put the egg yolks, vinegar and 2 teaspoons cold water in the Vita-Mix machine. Season lightly with salt and pepper and secure the 2-part lid. Select VARIABLE speed 1. Turn the machine on and increase the speed to 6. Run for 30 seconds or until frothy.
2 While the machine is still running, remove the lid plug and slowly add the hot, melted butter. Replace the lid plug and run for 5 minutes or until thick and creamy.
3 Remove the lid plug and add the tarragon. Run for 4–5 seconds until finely chopped, then stir in the lemon juice and cayenne pepper.
4 Bring a large, shallow pan of water to the boil. Break the eggs into a cup then slide them gently into the water. Reduce the heat to low and poach at a gentle simmer for 3–4 minutes. Remove with a slotted spoon and place on kitchen paper to drain.
5 Toast the muffin halves and then spread with a little butter. Top each muffin half with 1 slice of Parma ham and 1 poached egg. Pour over the hollandaise sauce and serve.

HEALTH BENEFITS • Energizing • Stress-busting • High protein • Low carb

Make this: *vegetarian by using smoked tofu or vegetarian ham instead of Parma ham.*

Scrambled Eggs with Vegetables

SERVES 4 **PREPARATION TIME:** 5 minutes **VITA-MIX TIME:** 7 minutes **COOKING TIME:** 4 minutes
SERVE WITH: Gluten-free or wholemeal toast **STORAGE:** Best eaten straight away.

6 tomatoes, halved • 1 tbsp vegetable oil • 8 large eggs • 3 tbsp full-fat milk • 300g/10½oz baby button mushrooms • salt and freshly ground black pepper

1 Preheat the grill to high. Put the tomatoes on a grill pan and drizzle with half the oil.
2 Put the eggs and milk in the Vita-Mix machine and season with salt and pepper. Secure the 2-part lid. Select VARIABLE speed 6 and run for 15 seconds, then increase to HIGH. Run for 6 minutes or until the sound of the motor changes as the eggs begin to solidify. At this stage, use the tamper to push the eggs into the blades and run for a further 30–45 seconds or until cooked through. Transfer to a bowl and mash the eggs with a fork.
3 While the eggs are scrambling, grill the tomatoes for 3–4 minutes until tender. Meanwhile, heat the remaining oil in a frying pan over a medium-high heat. Add the mushrooms and fry for 2–3 minutes, stirring frequently, until beginning to brown. Serve the tomatoes and mushrooms with the scrambled eggs.

HEALTH BENEFITS • Energizing • Stress-busting • High protein • Low carb

Make this: *dairy-free by using soya milk instead of full-fat milk or by omitting the milk.*

Vegetable Rosti with Smoked Salmon

SERVES 4 **PREPARATION TIME:** 10 minutes **VITA-MIX TIME:** 20 seconds
COOKING TIME: 20 minutes **STORAGE:** Leftovers can be kept in the fridge for up to 2 days. Reheat in a preheated oven at 180°C/350°F/Gas 4 for 5 minutes covered with foil.

Rosti 2 baking potatoes, peeled and cut into chunks • 2 carrots, peeled and cut into chunks
• 2 eggs, beaten • 2 tbsp olive oil • salt and freshly ground black pepper
Topping 125g/4½oz cream cheese • 1 small handful flat-leaf parsley • 1 tbsp lemon juice
• 150g/5½oz sliced smoked salmon

1 Put half of the potatoes and carrots in the Vita-Mix machine, cover with cold water and secure the 2-part lid. Select VARIABLE speed 3 and pulse on and off several times to chop finely, using the tamper to push the vegetables into the blades. The mixture should look coarsely grated. Be careful not to over-process or the vegetables will begin to purée. Drain the vegetables in a sieve, pressing them down with the back of a spoon to squeeze out any excess liquid, then transfer to a large bowl. Repeat with the remaining potatoes and carrots. Wash the Vita-Mix machine.
2 Add the eggs to the bowl, season with salt and pepper and mix well.
3 Heat the oil in a large non-stick frying pan over a medium heat. Put 3–4 tablespoons of the vegetable rosti mixture in the pan, spacing well apart and flattening each one with a spatula to form small rounds. Cook for 4–5 minutes on each side until cooked through and golden-brown. Transfer to a plate and repeat with the remaining mixture.
4 Put the cream cheese, parsley and lemon juice in the Vita-Mix machine and secure the 2-part lid. Select VARIABLE speed 2 and pulse on and off several times until the herbs are chopped and mixed with the cheese. Divide the rosti onto four serving plates and top each one with the herbed cheese and 1 slice of the smoked salmon. Serve immediately.

HEALTH BENEFITS • Energizing • Immune-boosting • Anti-ageing • Stress-busting • High protein

Lunches

Chicken Tortilla Wraps with Salsa Mexicana

Gazpacho

SERVES 4 **PREPARATION TIME:** 10 minutes **VITA-MIX TIME:** 50 seconds
STORAGE: Best served straight away, although it will keep in the fridge until the following day.
IF USING THE 32oz CONTAINER: Halve the quantities.

4 tomatoes, halved • 1 cucumber, peeled and chopped • 1 red pepper, quartered and deseeded
• ½ small red onion • 1 garlic clove • 1 dill sprig • ½ tsp paprika • 700ml/24fl oz tomato juice
• 2 tbsp olive oil • 2 tbsp lemon juice • dash of Tabasco sauce (optional) • 3 flat-leaf parsley sprigs
• salt and freshly ground black pepper

1 Put all the ingredients, except the parsley, in the Vita-Mix machine in the order listed and season with
salt and pepper. Secure the 2-part lid and select VARIABLE speed 1. Turn the machine on and increase
the speed to 10, then to HIGH. Run for 45 seconds or until well mixed and smooth.
2 Remove the lid plug and add the parsley. Replace the plug and pulse on and off several times until
the parsley is finely chopped and mixed in. Serve immediately.

HEALTH BENEFITS • Energizing • Detoxifying • Immune-boosting • Anti-ageing • Stress-busting
• Weight-shifting • High fibre • Low carb • Low cholesterol • Low saturated fat • Low calorie
• Low kilojoule

Chilled Melon & Yogurt Soup

SERVES 4 **PREPARATION TIME:** 5 minutes, plus 1 hour chilling **VITA-MIX TIME:** 15 seconds
SERVE WITH: Sun-dried Tomato & Black Olive Tapenade on Bruschetta (see page 86)
STORAGE: This will keep in the fridge for up to 3 days.
IF USING THE 32oz CONTAINER: Halve the quantities.

2 cantaloupe melons, peeled and deseeded • juice of 1 lime • 4 tbsp white wine • 5 tbsp natural yogurt
• 6 mint leaves, chopped

1 Put the melon, lime juice and wine in the Vita-Mix machine, secure the 2-part lid and select VARIABLE
speed 3. Turn the machine on and increase the speed to 10, then to HIGH. Run for 10 seconds until
smooth. Switch off the machine, add the yogurt and select VARIABLE speed 3.
2 Run for 4–5 seconds until well mixed. Transfer to a bowl, cover and chill for 1 hour.
3 Spoon the soup into bowls, sprinkle over the mint and serve.

HEALTH BENEFITS • Energizing • Immune-boosting • Anti-ageing • Weight-shifting • Low cholesterol
• Low saturated fat • Low calorie • Low kilojoule

*Make this: dairy-free by using soya yogurt instead of natural yogurt or by omitting the yogurt
completely. For a sugar-free version, omit the wine.*

Borscht

SERVES 4 **PREPARATION TIME:** 15 minutes **VITA-MIX TIME:** 3 minutes 5 seconds
COOKING TIME: 30 minutes **STORAGE:** Best served straight away, although it will keep in an airtight
container in the fridge for up to 1 day. **IF USING THE 32oz CONTAINER:** Halve the quantities.

8 beetroot, peeled and quartered • 800ml/28fl oz vegetable stock • 1 bay leaf • 100g/3½oz red cabbage,
chopped • 1 red pepper, quartered and deseeded • ½ green pepper, quartered and deseeded
• 2 carrots, peeled and halved • 5 radishes, trimmed • ½ celery stick • 1 shallot • 2 garlic cloves
• juice of ½ lemon • 1 tbsp olive oil • 1 handful flat-leaf parsley • 4 tbsp soured cream
• salt and freshly ground black pepper

1 Put the beetroot, stock and bay leaf in a saucepan. Bring to the boil over a high heat, then reduce the heat
  to medium and simmer, covered, for 30 minutes until the beetroot are tender.
2 Transfer the beetroot, stock and bay leaf to the Vita-Mix machine. Add the cabbage, peppers, carrots,
  radishes, celery, shallot, garlic, lemon juice and oil and season with salt and pepper. Secure the 2-part lid
  and select VARIABLE speed 1. Turn the machine on and increase the speed to 10, then to HIGH. Run for
  2–3 minutes until smooth.
3 Remove the lid plug and add the parsley and soured cream. Replace the plug and pulse on and off several
  times until the parsley is finely chopped. Serve immediately.

HEALTH BENEFITS • Energizing • Detoxifying • Immune-boosting • Anti-ageing • Stress-busting
• Weight-shifting • High fibre • Low carb • Low cholesterol • Low saturated fat • Low calorie
• Low kilojoule

Make this: citrus-free by omitting the lemon juice.

Roasted Tomato & Red Pepper Soup

SERVES 4 **PREPARATION TIME:** 10 minutes **VITA-MIX TIME:** 5 minutes **COOKING TIME:** 20 minutes
STORAGE: Best served straight away, although it will keep in the fridge until the following day.
IF USING THE 32oz CONTAINER: Halve the quantities.

5 tomatoes, halved • 2 red peppers, quartered and deseeded • 2 tbsp olive oil • 1 onion, chopped
• 1 small garlic clove • 1 carrot, peeled and halved • 1 tbsp tomato purée • 500ml/17fl oz vegetable
stock • 2 basil sprigs • ½ tsp paprika

1 Preheat the oven to 200°C/400°F/Gas 6. Put the tomatoes and peppers in a baking dish, add
   1 tablespoon of the oil and mix well. Bake for 20 minutes, stirring occasionally, until tender.
2 Meanwhile, heat the remaining oil in a frying pan over a medium heat. Add the onion and fry for
   4–5 minutes, stirring occasionally, until soft.
3 Transfer the tomatoes, peppers and onion to the Vita-Mix machine. Add the garlic, carrot, tomato
   purée, stock, basil and paprika. Secure the 2-part lid and select VARIABLE speed 1. Turn the machine
   on and increase the speed to 10, then to HIGH. Run for about 4–5 minutes or until smooth and
   steaming. Serve immediately.

HEALTH BENEFITS • Energizing • Detoxifying • Immune-boosting • Anti-ageing • Stress-busting
• Weight-shifting • High fibre • Low carb • Low cholesterol • Low saturated fat • Low calorie
• Low kilojoule

Potato & Fennel Soup with Dill

SERVES 4 **PREPARATION TIME:** 10 minutes **VITA-MIX TIME:** 5 minutes **COOKING TIME:** 15 minutes
STORAGE: Best served straight away, although it will keep in the fridge until the following day.
IF USING THE 32oz CONTAINER: Halve the quantities.

3 potatoes, peeled and diced • 1 shallot, halved • 1 fennel bulb with leaves, quartered
• 1 celery stick, chopped • 1 small garlic clove • 1 handful dill • 600ml/21fl oz vegetable stock
• 200ml/7fl oz semi-skimmed milk

1 Bring a saucepan of water to the boil. Add the potatoes and cook for 15 minutes until soft, then drain
and transfer to the Vita-Mix machine.
2 Add the remaining ingredients in the order listed and secure the 2-part lid. Select VARIABLE speed 1.
Turn the machine on and increase the speed to 10, then to HIGH. Run for 4–5 minutes or until smooth
and steaming. Serve immediately.

HEALTH BENEFITS • Energizing • Detoxifying • Immune boosting • Anti-ageing • Stress busting
• Weight-shifting • High fibre • Low cholesterol • Low saturated fat • Low calorie • Low kilojoule

Make this: *vegan and dairy-free by using soya milk instead of semi-skimmed milk.*

Spring Vegetable Soup

SERVES 4 **PREPARATION TIME:** 10 minutes **VITA-MIX TIME:** 5 minutes **COOKING TIME:** 20 minutes
STORAGE: Best served straight away, although it will keep in the fridge until the following day.
IF USING THE 32oz CONTAINER: Halve the quantities.

400g/14oz baby new potatoes, halved • 2 dried bay leaves • 5 tbsp fresh shelled peas • 2 spring onions,
halved • 8 baby carrots • 1 garlic clove • 2 flat-leaf parsley sprigs • ¼ tsp dried thyme • ¼ tsp dried
oregano • 1 tsp olive oil • 600ml/21fl oz vegetable stock • salt and freshly ground black pepper

1 Put the potatoes and bay leaves in a steamer and steam for 15 minutes until starting to soften. Add the
peas and steam for a further 5 minutes until the vegetables are tender.
2 Transfer the steamed vegetables and bay leaves to the Vita-Mix machine and add the remaining ingredients
in the order listed, then season with salt and pepper. Secure the 2-part lid and select VARIABLE speed 1.
Turn the machine on and increase the speed to 10, then to HIGH. Run for 4–5 minutes or until smooth
and steaming. Serve immediately.

HEALTH BENEFITS • Energizing • Detoxifying • Immune-boosting • Anti-ageing • Stress-busting
• Weight-shifting • High fibre • Low cholesterol • Low saturated fat • Low calorie • Low kilojoule

Butternut Squash & Coconut Soup

SERVES 4 **PREPARATION TIME:** 10 minutes **VITA-MIX TIME:** 4 minutes **COOKING TIME:** 45 minutes
STORAGE: Best served straight away, although it will keep in the fridge until the following day.
IF USING THE 32oz CONTAINER: Halve the quantities.

1 butternut squash, halved lengthways and deseeded • 1 tbsp olive oil • 1 small garlic clove
• 3 chives • 2cm/¾in piece green chilli, deseeded • 1 carrot, peeled and quartered • 150ml/5fl oz coconut milk • 600ml/21fl oz vegetable stock • 1 tbsp lime juice • a pinch saffron

1 Preheat the oven to 220°C/425°F/Gas 7. Brush the squash with the olive oil and put it face-down on a baking sheet. Bake for 45 minutes or until soft.
2 Scoop out the squash flesh and put it in the Vita-Mix machine along with the remaining ingredients in the order listed. Secure the 2-part lid and select VARIABLE speed 1. Turn the machine on and increase the speed to 10, then to HIGH. Run for 3–4 minutes or until smooth and steaming. Serve immediately.

HEALTH BENEFITS • Energizing • Immune-boosting • Anti-ageing • Stress-busting • Weight-shifting
• High fibre • Low cholesterol • Low saturated fat • Low calorie • Low kilojoule

Tomato, Haricot Bean & Chilli Soup

SERVES 4 **PREPARATION TIME:** 10 minutes, plus optional overnight soaking
VITA-MIX TIME: 5 minutes **COOKING TIME:** 2 hours if using dried beans; 15 minutes if using tinned
STORAGE: Best served straight away, although it will keep in the fridge for up to 1 day.
IF USING THE 32oz CONTAINER: Halve the quantities.

200g/7oz dried haricot beans, soaked in water overnight and drained or 400g/14oz tinned haricot beans, drained and rinsed • 1 large sweet potato, peeled and chopped • 1 tbsp olive oil • 1 onion, chopped
• 3 tomatoes, halved • 2 tbsp tomato purée • 3 garlic cloves • ½ red pepper, deseeded • ¼ red chilli, deseeded • ½ tsp paprika • 700ml/24fl oz vegetable stock • salt and freshly ground black pepper

1 If using dried beans, put them in a saucepan and cover with water. Bring to the boil over a high heat, then reduce the heat to medium-low and simmer, covered, for 2 hours or until soft. Drain and set aside.
2 Meanwhile, put the sweet potato in a steamer and steam for 15 minutes until tender. Heat the oil in a frying pan over a medium heat. Add the onion and cook for 4–5 minutes until soft.
3 Put the beans, sweet potato and onion in the Vita-Mix machine along with the remaining ingredients in the order listed and season with salt and pepper. Secure the 2-part lid and select VARIABLE speed 1. Turn the machine on and increase the speed to 10, then to HIGH. Run for 5 minutes or until smooth and steaming. Serve immediately.

HEALTH BENEFITS • Energizing • Immune-boosting • Anti-ageing • Stress-busting • Weight-shifting
• High protein • High fibre • Low cholesterol • Low saturated fat • Low calorie • Low kilojoule

French Watercress Soup

SERVES 4 **PREPARATION TIME:** 5 minutes **VITA-MIX TIME:** 4 minutes **COOKING TIME:** 3 minutes
STORAGE: Best served straight away, although it will keep in the fridge until the following day.
IF USING THE 32oz CONTAINER: Halve the quantities.

1 tbsp olive oil • 1 onion, chopped • 1 small garlic clove • 1 celery stick, chopped
• 100g/3½oz watercress • 1 thyme sprig • 1 tsp lemon juice • 500ml/17fl oz vegetable stock
• 100ml/3½fl oz single cream • salt and freshly ground black pepper

1 Heat the oil in a frying pan over a medium-high heat. Add the onion and cook for 2–3 minutes, stirring occasionally, until soft.
2 Transfer the onion to the Vita-Mix machine. Add the remaining ingredients in the order listed and season with salt and pepper. Secure the 2-part lid and select VARIABLE speed 1. Turn the machine on and increase the speed to 10, then to HIGH. Run for 3–4 minutes or until smooth and steaming. Serve immediately.

HEALTH BENEFITS • Energizing • Immune-boosting • Anti-ageing • Stress-busting • Weight-shifting
• Low carb • Low calorie • Low kilojoule

Quick Miso Fish Soup

SERVES 4 **PREPARATION TIME:** 10 minutes **VITA-MIX TIME:** 15 seconds
COOKING TIME: 3 minutes **STORAGE:** Will keep in the fridge for up to 2 days.
IF USING THE 32oz CONTAINER: Halve the quantities.

3 spring onions • 55g/2oz instant miso soup powder • 1cm/½in piece root ginger, peeled
• 100g/3½oz shiitake mushrooms, stalks removed • 200g/7oz pak choi, shredded • 125g/4½oz rice
noodles • 1 tbsp tamari • 200g/7oz skinless white fish fillet, such as cod or pollack, cut into cubes
• a few coriander leaves

1 Put the spring onions in the Vita-Mix machine and secure the 2-part lid. Select VARIABLE speed 1
  and pulse on and off 2–3 times to chop. Transfer to a bowl and set aside.
2 Put the miso soup, ginger and 800ml/28fl oz water in the Vita-Mix machine and secure the 2-part lid.
  Select VARIABLE speed 3. Turn the machine on and increase the speed to 10, then to HIGH. Run for
  10 seconds to combine. Add the mushrooms. Select VARIABLE speed 1 and pulse on and off 2–3 times
  until coarsely chopped.
3 Transfer the soup to a pan, add the pak choi, noodles, tamari and fish. Simmer over a medium heat
  for 3 minutes or until the noodles are tender and the fish is cooked. Sprinkle with the coriander leaves
  and serve immediately.

HEALTH BENEFITS • Immune-boosting • Anti-ageing • Stress-busting • Weight-shifting
• Low cholesterol • Low saturated fat • Low calorie • Low kilojoule

Prawn & Coconut Laksa

SERVES 4 **PREPARATION TIME:** 10 minutes **VITA-MIX TIME:** 6 minutes **COOKING TIME:** 5 minutes
STORAGE: Best served straight away, although it will keep in the fridge for up to 2 days.
IF USING THE 32oz CONTAINER: Halve the quantities.

2 shallots • 1 red chilli, deseeded • 2 garlic cloves • 2cm/¾in piece root ginger, peeled • ½ tsp ground
coriander • 6 coriander sprigs • 3 tomatoes, quartered • 400ml/14fl oz coconut milk • 1 tbsp cornflour
• 2 tbsp Thai fish sauce • 1 tsp sesame oil • 1 red pepper, quartered and deseeded • 20 peeled large raw
prawns • 3 tbsp finely chopped mint • 200g/7oz dried rice noodles • 3 spring onions, chopped
• 1 lime, quartered, to serve

1 Put the shallots, chilli, garlic, ginger and ground and fresh coriander in the Vita-Mix machine and secure
the 2-part lid. Select VARIABLE speed 3 and run for about 5–6 seconds to form a coarse paste. Remove
the lid plug and add the tomatoes, coconut milk and cornflour. Replace the lid plug. Turn the machine
on and increase the speed to 10, then to HIGH. Run for about 5 minutes until a thick sauce is produced.
2 Decrease the speed to 2 and, with the machine running, add the fish sauce, sesame oil and red
pepper through the lid plug opening. Replace the lid plug and pulse on and off a few times until the
pepper is chopped.
3 Pour the sauce into a pan and add the prawns. Simmer for 3–4 minutes until the prawns turn pink
and are cooked through. Stir in the chopped mint leaves.
4 Meanwhile, cook the rice noodles according to the packet instructions.
5 Divide the noodles into four large bowls and ladle the spicy prawn soup over them. Sprinkle the spring
onions over the top and serve immediately, garnished with the lime wedges.

HEALTH BENEFITS • Energizing • Immune-boosting • Anti-ageing • High protein

Chicken, Onion & Chorizo Soup

SERVES 4 **PREPARATION TIME:** 10 minutes **VITA-MIX TIME:** 3 minutes **COOKING TIME:** 12 minutes
SERVE WITH: Gluten-free rice cakes, or wholemeal or rye bread **STORAGE:** This will keep in the fridge
for up to 2 days.

2 red onions • 1 tbsp olive oil • 150g/5½oz chorizo sausage, skin removed, cut into bite-sized pieces
• 1 skinless, boneless chicken breast, diced • 3 thyme sprigs • 1 garlic clove • 1 leek • 2 carrots
• 1l/35fl oz chicken stock • 2 tbsp chopped flat-leaf parsley

1 Put 1 of the onions in the Vita-Mix machine and secure the 2-part lid. Select VARIABLE speed 1 and pulse
on and off to chop. Remove from the container.
2 Heat the oil in a heavy-based pan and lightly fry the chorizo, chicken, chopped onion and thyme sprigs,
stirring over a medium heat for 10 minutes or until the chicken is cooked through.
3 Put the remaining onion and the garlic, leek and carrots in the Vita-Mix machine with the chicken stock
and secure the 2-part lid. Select VARIABLE speed 3. Turn the machine on and increase the speed to 10,
then to HIGH. Run for 2–3 minutes until the soup is hot. Switch off the machine and pour the soup into
the pan with the chorizo and chicken mixture. Simmer over a medium heat for 1–2 minutes until heated
through. Sprinkle the parsley over and serve immediately.

HEALTH BENEFITS • Energizing • Stress-busting • High protein • Low carb

Split Pea & Ham Soup

SERVES 4 **PREPARATION TIME:** 10 minutes **VITA-MIX TIME:** 3 minutes 20 seconds
COOKING TIME: 45 minutes **SERVE WITH:** Wholemeal or rye bread
STORAGE: This will keep in the fridge for up to 3 days. Can also be frozen without the ham for up to 1 month. **IF USING THE 32oz CONTAINER:** Halve the quantities.

200g/7oz yellow split peas • 1.25l/44fl oz vegetable stock • 1 bay leaf • 1 garlic clove • 6 mint leaves • 1 celery stick • ½ onion • 1 carrot • 1 tbsp sherry vinegar • 1 tsp Dijon mustard • 150ml/5fl oz beer • 110g/3¾oz cooked ham from the bone, diced • 2 tbsp chopped flat-leaf parsley, for sprinkling • salt and freshly ground black pepper

1 Put the split peas, stock, bay leaf, garlic and mint leaves in a large saucepan. Simmer over a medium heat for 45 minutes until the peas soften. Remove the bay leaf.
2 Put the celery, onion and carrot in the Vita-Mix machine and add the split peas and liquid. Secure the 2-part lid and select VARIABLE speed 3. Turn the machine on and gradually increase the speed to 10, then to HIGH. Run for 10–20 seconds until thoroughly blended. Add the vinegar, mustard and beer. Select VARIABLE speed 3. Turn the machine on and increase the speed to 10, then to HIGH. Run for 2–3 minutes until smooth and heated through.
3 Season with salt and pepper, then stir in the ham. Sprinkle with the parsley and serve immediately.

HEALTH BENEFITS • Energizing • Stress-busting • High protein • High fibre • Low carb • Low cholesterol • Low saturated fat

Pork Wonton Soup

SERVES 4 **PREPARATION TIME:** 15 minutes **VITA-MIX TIME:** 17 seconds
COOKING TIME: 10 minutes **STORAGE:** Leftovers will keep in the fridge until the following day.
IF USING THE 32oz CONTAINER: Halve the quantities.

4 spring onions • 1cm/½in piece root ginger, peeled • 1 garlic clove • 150g/5½oz pork fillet, cut into chunks • 1 tbsp rice wine • 2 tbsp tamari • 16 wonton wrappers • 875ml/30fl oz chicken stock • 150g/5½oz pak choi, shredded • 60g/2¼oz tinned sweetcorn • 75g/2½oz bean sprouts • 2 tbsp chopped coriander leaves

1 Put 1 of the spring onions, the ginger and garlic in the Vita-Mix machine and secure the 2-part lid. Select VARIABLE speed 3 and run for 3–4 seconds until finely chopped. Add the pork fillet, rice wine and 1 tablespoon of the tamari. Select VARIABLE speed 3 and run for 8–9 seconds until the mixture forms a paste. Transfer to a bowl and wash the Vita-Mix machine.
2 Put 1 wonton wrapper on a clean work surface. Brush lightly with water and put 1 teaspoon of the pork filling in the centre. Shape into a money bag by bringing all the edges together in the centre, sealing well. Repeat with the remaining wrappers and filling.
3 Put the stock in a large saucepan and bring to a simmer over a medium heat. Add the wontons and cook for 3–4 minutes until the wrappers have softened and expanded in size. Work in batches, if necessary, to avoid overcrowding the pan.
4 Put the remaining spring onions in the Vita-Mix machine and secure the 2-part lid. Select VARIABLE speed 1 and run for 3–4 seconds to chop coarsely. Add them to the stock, along with the pak choi and sweetcorn. Simmer for a further 1 minute. Add the remaining tamari to taste and the bean sprouts. Sprinkle with the coriander leaves and serve immediately.

HEALTH BENEFITS • Energizing • Immune-boosting • Stress-busting

Sweet Potato
& Sun-Dried Tomato Fritters

SERVES 4 **PREPARATION TIME:** 5 minutes **VITA-MIX TIME:** 40 seconds **COOKING TIME:** 12 minutes
SERVE WITH: Yogurt raita and watercress **STORAGE:** These will keep in the fridge for up to 3 days.

350g/12oz sweet potatoes, peeled and quartered • 4 sun-dried tomatoes in oil, drained
• 1 handful basil leaves • salt and freshly ground black pepper
Batter 1 egg • 40g/1½oz plain flour • 40g/1½oz cornflour • a pinch cayenne pepper • 4 tbsp olive oil

1 Put the sweet potatoes in the Vita-Mix machine and secure the 2-part lid. Select VARIABLE speed 1. Turn
the machine on and run for 5–6 seconds, then scrape down the sides and run for a further 5–6 seconds
until coarsely chopped. Add the tomatoes and basil leaves and turn the machine on again. Increase the
speed to 6 and run for 4–5 seconds until a coarse mixture forms, using the tamper to press the vegetables
into the blades. Put the vegetables in a bowl and season with salt and pepper. Wash the Vita-Mix machine.

2 Put the egg, flour, cornflour, cayenne pepper and 125ml/4fl oz cold water in the Vita-Mix machine and
secure the 2-part lid. Select VARIABLE speed 1, turn the machine on and increase the speed to 10, then
to HIGH. Run for 10–20 seconds, then add the batter to the vegetables and mix well.

3 Heat the oil in a frying pan over a medium-high heat. Using a slotted spoon, take tablespoons of the
mixture, letting the excess batter drip back into the bowl, and fry them 3–4 at a time for 2 minutes on
each side, flattening each one in the pan. Remove and drain on kitchen paper. Repeat with the remaining
batter to make 12 fritters, then serve.

HEALTH BENEFITS • Immune-boosting • High fibre • Low cholesterol • Low saturated fat

Make this: *wheat- and gluten-free by using gluten-free flour mix or rice flour instead of plain flour.*

Asparagus Tofu Quiche

SERVES 4 **PREPARATION TIME:** 20 minutes, plus 20 minutes resting
VITA-MIX TIME: 1 minute **COOKING TIME:** 1 hour **SERVE WITH:** A tomato salad
STORAGE: Leftovers will keep in the fridge for up to 2 days.

Pastry sunflower oil, for greasing • 100g/3½oz plain flour, plus extra for rolling the dough
• a pinch salt • 50g/1¾oz vegetable margarine
Filling 375g/13oz firm tofu, diced • 200ml/7fl oz soya milk • 1 tbsp olive oil • 1 tbsp soy sauce
• ½ small onion • 1 garlic clove • 1 tsp dried mixed herbs • 1 tsp paprika • ½ tsp mustard powder
• ½ tsp vegetable bouillon powder • 70g/2½oz asparagus tips • salt and freshly ground black pepper

1 Grease a 20cm/8in round flan dish with oil. Put the flour, salt and margarine in a mixing bowl and rub
  together until the mixture resembles breadcrumbs. Add 3 tablespoons cold water and mix into a dough.
  Cover and leave to rest for 20 minutes.
2 Preheat the oven to 190°C/375°F/Gas 5. On a lightly floured surface, roll the pastry out and put it in the
  oiled dish. Bake for 10–15 minutes, then set aside.
3 Put all the ingredients for the filling, except the asparagus, in the Vita-Mix machine. Season with salt and
  pepper, secure the 2-part lid and select VARIABLE speed 1. Turn the machine on and increase the speed
  to 10, then to HIGH. Run for 1 minute or until smooth. Spoon the filling into the pastry case.
4 Bring a pan of water to the boil. Add the asparagus tips and cook for 1 minute, then drain. Arrange the
  asparagus on top of the quiche, pressing gently. Bake for 40 minutes until set, then serve hot or cold.

HEALTH BENEFITS • Energizing • Immune-boosting • Anti-ageing • Stress-busting • Weight-shifting
• High protein • High fibre • Low carb • Low cholesterol • Low saturated fat • Low calorie
• Low kilojoule

Make this: gluten-free by using an all-purpose gluten-free flour instead of wheat flour and tamari
instead of soy sauce.

Sesame Falafel

SERVES 4 **PREPARATION TIME:** 10 minutes, plus overnight soaking and 30 minutes resting
VITA-MIX TIME: 1 minute 10 seconds **COOKING TIME:** 1 hour 40 minutes
SERVE WITH: Lemon, Coriander & Green Olive Hummus (see page 84) and a leafy green salad
STORAGE: This can be kept in the fridge for 2 to 3 days or frozen for up to 1 month.

150g/5½oz dried chickpeas, soaked in water overnight and drained • 2 garlic cloves • ½ small onion, chopped • 55g/2oz sesame seeds • ½ tsp ground cumin • ½ tsp chilli powder • 1 tsp tamari • 100ml/3½fl oz vegetable stock • 1 handful flat-leaf parsley • 50g/1¾oz rice flour • 4½ tsp arrowroot • 500ml/17fl oz vegetable oil, for deep-frying • salt and freshly ground black pepper

1 Put the chickpeas in a large saucepan, cover with water and bring to the boil over a high heat. Reduce the heat to medium and simmer, covered, for 1½ hours or until soft, then drain.
2 Put the chickpeas, garlic, onion, sesame seeds, cumin, chilli powder, tamari and stock in the Vita-Mix machine. Secure the 2-part lid and select VARIABLE speed 1. Turn the machine on and increase the speed to 6. Run for 1 minute or until well mixed, using the tamper to push the ingredients into the blades.
3 With the machine still running, remove the lid plug and add the parsley. Replace the plug and run for a further 10 seconds or until the parsley is finely chopped and evenly distributed. Transfer the mixture to a large bowl. Add the rice flour and arrowroot and season with salt and pepper. Mix well and leave to rest for 30 minutes. Shape the mixture into 12 balls, then flatten slightly.
4 Heat the oil in a small, deep frying pan and, working in batches, deep-fry the falafel for 3 minutes, turning occasionally, until browned. Remove with a slotted spoon and drain on kitchen paper, then serve.

HEALTH BENEFITS • Energizing • High protein • High fibre • Low carb • Low cholesterol • Stress-busting

Mexican Tofu
& Red Pepper Croquettes

SERVES 4 **PREPARATION TIME:** 10 minutes **VITA-MIX TIME:** 35 seconds
COOKING TIME: 1 hour **STORAGE:** This can be kept in the fridge for 2 to 3 days or frozen for up to 1 month.

150g/5½oz short-grain brown rice • 250g/9oz firm tofu, diced • ½ red pepper, deseeded and quartered • ½ celery stick, chopped • ¼ onion • 1 garlic clove • 1 tbsp tomato purée • 1 tsp paprika • ½ tsp chilli powder • 1 tbsp tamari • 1 handful coriander leaves • 3–4 tbsp olive oil (optional) • salt and freshly ground black pepper

1 Put the rice and 750ml/26fl oz water in a saucepan. Bring to the boil and simmer, covered, for 45 minutes until the rice is soft and all the water has been absorbed. Leave to cool, then transfer to a large bowl.
2 Meanwhile, put the tofu, red pepper, celery, onion, garlic, tomato purée, paprika, chilli powder and tamari in the Vita-Mix machine. Season with salt and pepper and secure the 2-part lid. Select VARIABLE speed 6 and run for 30 seconds or until well mixed, using the tamper to push the ingredients into the blades.
3 With the machine still running, remove the lid plug and add the coriander leaves. Replace the lid plug and pulse on and off several times until finely chopped and well mixed. Add the tofu mixture to the brown rice and mix well.
4 Preheat the grill to low. Shape the mixture into 12 balls, then flatten slightly and put them on a grill pan.
5 Grill for 8 minutes on each side until golden brown. Alternatively, heat the olive oil in a frying pan over a medium-high heat and fry the croquettes a few at a time for 4 minutes on each side until golden brown. Serve warm.

HEALTH BENEFITS • Energizing • Detoxifying • Immune-boosting • Anti-ageing • Stress-busting • Weight-shifting • High fibre • Low cholesterol • Low saturated fat • Low calorie • Low kilojoule

Tomato Pesto & Black Olive Pizza

SERVES 4 **PREPARATION TIME:** 30 minutes, plus 1 hour rising
VITA-MIX TIME: 35 seconds **COOKING TIME:** 15 minutes **SERVE WITH:** A large mixed salad
STORAGE: The pesto can be made in advance and kept in the fridge for up to 5 days. Leftovers will keep in the fridge for up to 2 days.

Pizza base 175g/6oz plain flour, plus extra for kneading the dough • a pinch salt • 1 tsp dried active yeast • 1 tbsp olive oil
Pesto 100g/3½oz pine nuts • 4–5 sun-dried tomatoes in oil, drained • 20g/¾ oz basil leaves
• 1 small garlic clove • 125ml/4fl oz olive oil • 1 tbsp lemon juice • salt and freshly ground black pepper
Topping 5 tomatoes, sliced • 85g/3oz pitted black olives, sliced • 140g/5oz mozzarella cheese, drained and sliced

1 Sift the flour into a large bowl and add the salt and yeast. Make a well in the centre and add the oil and 125ml/4fl oz lukewarm water. Mix well to form a soft dough, adding more water if required. Turn the dough out onto a lightly floured surface and knead for 8 minutes or until smooth and elastic. Transfer to a clean bowl, cover and leave to rise for 1 hour.
2 Meanwhile, make the pesto. Put the pine nuts in a dry, heavy-based pan over a medium-low heat and cook for 3 minutes, stirring frequently, until lightly golden. Transfer the pine nuts to the Vita-Mix machine and add the remaining pesto ingredients in the order listed. Season with salt and pepper and secure the 2-part lid. Select VARIABLE speed 5 and run for 35 seconds or until blended.
3 Preheat the oven to 220°C/425°F/Gas 7. Knock back the dough and knead it again on a lightly floured surface for 2–3 minutes, then roll it out into a 30cm/12in circle and put on a baking sheet. Spread the pesto over the pizza base, then arrange the tomatoes and olives on top. Dot with the mozzarella and bake for 15 minutes or until the cheese has melted and the pizza is cooked. Serve immediately.

HEALTH BENEFITS • Energizing • High protein

Make this: high-fibre by using wholemeal flour for the pizza base instead of white flour.

Three-Cheese & Spinach Frittata

SERVES 4 **PREPARATION TIME:** 10 minutes **VITA-MIX TIME:** 12 seconds
COOKING TIME: 12 minutes **SERVE WITH:** Grilled tomatoes and buttered wholemeal rolls
STORAGE: Best eaten straight away.

4 large eggs • 3 tbsp double cream • 100g/3½oz mixed cheese, such as Cheddar, Cheshire and feta or any 3 cheeses of choice, diced • 1 garlic clove • 3 tbsp vegetable oil • 150g/5½oz baby spinach leaves
• 5g/⅛oz chives • 1 dill sprig • 1 tarragon sprig, leaves only • 3 basil leaves
• salt and freshly ground black pepper

1 Put the eggs, cream, cheese and garlic in the Vita-Mix machine and season with salt and pepper. Secure the 2-part lid and select VARIABLE speed 1. Turn the machine on and increase to the speed to 6. Run for 8 seconds or until well mixed. Set aside.
2 Heat 1 tablespoon of the oil in a large pan over a medium heat. Add the spinach, chives, dill, tarragon and basil, cover and cook for 3 minutes or until the spinach has wilted.
3 Preheat the grill to high. Add the spinach and herbs to the egg mixture in the Vita-Mix machine and secure the 2-part lid. Select VARIABLE speed 3 and pulse on and off a few times until chopped.
4 Heat the remaining oil in a large ovenproof frying pan over a medium heat. Add the egg mixture and cook until it begins to set around the edges, pushing any uncooked egg to exposed parts of the pan. Once it has set underneath, put the pan under the grill for 5 minutes or until the top is cooked and golden. Cut the frittata into wedges and serve.

HEALTH BENEFITS • Energizing • High protein • Low carb • Stress-busting

Spaghetti with Anchovy, Olive & Tomato Sauce

SERVES 4 **PREPARATION TIME:** 10 minutes **VITA-MIX TIME:** 3 minutes
COOKING TIME: 12 minutes **SERVE WITH:** A leafy green salad
STORAGE: Prepare the sauce in advance and keep in the fridge for up to 2 days.

400g/14oz wholemeal spaghetti • 1 red onion • 1 garlic clove • a pinch dried chilli flakes
• 450g/1lb tomatoes, chopped • 4 sun-dried tomatoes in oil, drained • 100g/3½oz green pitted olives,
sliced • 4 tinned anchovy fillets in oil, rinsed and chopped • 2 tbsp capers, drained • 2 tbsp chopped basil
leaves • 3 tbsp grated Parmesan cheese • freshly ground black pepper

1 Bring a large pan of water to the boil. Add the spaghetti and cook according to the packet instructions
   until al dente, about 8–10 minutes, then drain.
2 Meanwhile, put the onion, garlic, dried chilli flakes, tomatoes and sun-dried tomatoes in the Vita-Mix
   machine and secure the 2-part lid. Select VARIABLE speed 3. Turn the machine on and increase the speed
   to 10, then to HIGH. Run for 2–3 minutes until the sauce is warm. Transfer the sauce to a pan.
3 Add the olives, anchovies and capers to the sauce and simmer over a medium-low heat for 1–2 minutes,
   stirring occasionally, until well mixed and warmed through.
4 Add the spaghetti to the sauce, then add the basil and toss to coat. Season with pepper, sprinkle with
   the Parmesan and serve immediately.

HEALTH BENEFITS • Immune-boosting • Anti-ageing • Stress-busting • High fibre

Salmon Fish Cakes with Dill Aioli

SERVES 4 **PREPARATION TIME:** 20 minutes, plus 1 hour chilling **VITA-MIX TIME:** 45 seconds
COOKING TIME: 30 minutes **SERVE WITH:** Fennel Coleslaw in Tofu Dressing (see page 93)
STORAGE: Make the aioli in advance and keep chilled for up to 1 day. Leftover fish cakes will keep
for up to 1 day. The fish cakes can be frozen uncooked for up to 1 month.

Dill aioli 2 egg yolks • 1 tsp Dijon mustard • 4 dill sprigs • 1–2 tbsp lemon juice • 200ml/7fl oz olive oil
Fish cakes 500g/1lb 2oz floury potatoes, peeled and chopped • 15g/½oz butter • 4 spring onions
• 2 flat-leaf parsley sprigs • 2 dill sprigs • zest of 1 lemon • 500g/1lb 2oz skinless salmon fillet,
cut into chunks • 3–4 slices of bread • 1 egg, beaten • 2 tbsp olive oil • freshly ground black pepper

1 To make the dill aioli, put the egg yolks, mustard, dill and lemon juice in the Vita-Mix machine and secure
   the 2-part lid. Select VARIABLE speed 3 and run for 7–8 seconds. With the machine still running, slowly
   pour in the oil and blend for 10 seconds or until thick. Transfer the aioli to a bowl, cover and chill until
   required. Wash the Vita-Mix machine.
2 Put the potatoes in a pan of boiling water and cook for 10–12 minutes until tender. Drain well.
3 Put the potatoes and butter in the Vita-Mix machine and secure the 2-part lid. Select VARIABLE speed 6
   and run for 5–6 seconds until thick and smooth, using the tamper to press the potatoes into the blades
   if necessary. Transfer to a large bowl.
4 Put the spring onions, parsley, dill and lemon zest in the Vita-Mix machine and secure the 2-part lid. Select
   VARIABLE speed 3 and pulse on and off to chop finely. Add the salmon and run for 6–7 seconds or until
   a chunky paste forms. Stir into the potatoes and season with pepper. Wash the Vita-Mix machine.
5 Put the bread in the Vita-Mix machine and secure the 2-part lid. Select VARIABLE speed 3 and run for
   4–5 seconds, then switch to HIGH and run for a further 3–4 seconds to form fine breadcrumbs, using
   the tamper to press the bread into the blades. Transfer to a plate.
6 Shape the salmon mixture into 8 cakes of equal size. Dip each cake into the beaten egg, then coat in the
   breadcrumbs. Put the cakes on a plate, cover with cling film and chill for 1 hour.
7 Heat the oil in a frying pan over a medium-high heat. Working in batches, cook the fish cakes for 3–4
   minutes on each side until golden brown. Alternatively, preheat the oven to 200°C/400°F/Gas 6 and bake
   the cakes for 20 minutes until golden brown and cooked through, turning half way through cooking.
   Serve warm with the dill aioli.

HEALTH BENEFITS • Energizing • Immune-boosting • Stress-busting • High protein

Make this: *wheat- and gluten-free by using polenta to coat the fish cakes instead of breadcrumbs.*

Crab Cakes with
Sweet Chilli Dipping Sauce

SERVES 4 **PREPARATION TIME:** 15 minutes, plus 30 minutes chilling
VITA-MIX TIME: 1 minute 20 seconds **COOKING TIME:** 8 minutes
SERVE WITH: A leafy green salad or Fennel Coleslaw in Tofu Dressing (see page 93)
STORAGE: The dipping sauce can be made in advance and kept in the fridge for up to 2 days. Leftover crab cakes will keep in the fridge for up to 2 days.

Crab cakes 4 slices of bread • 1 red pepper, quartered and deseeded • 2 spring onions, halved
• 400g/14oz white crabmeat • zest of 1 lime • 1 tbsp lime juice • a pinch cayenne pepper
• 3 coriander sprigs • a dash of Tabasco sauce • 2 tbsp mayonnaise • 3 tbsp olive oil
• salt and freshly ground black pepper
Dipping sauce 2 tomatoes, halved • 110g/3¾oz caster sugar • 6 tbsp rice wine vinegar
• 2 red chillies, deseeded • 2 garlic cloves • 1 tbsp lime juice • 1 tbsp Thai fish sauce

1 To make the crab cakes, secure the 2-part lid on the Vita-Mix machine and select VARIABLE speed 2. Turn the machine on and, with the lid plug removed, feed the bread into the container, using the tamper to push it into the blades. Run for 5 seconds or until it has formed breadcrumbs. Transfer to a bowl and set aside.
2 Put the red pepper and spring onions in the Vita-Mix machine and secure the 2-part lid. Select VARIABLE speed 2 and pulse on and off a few times until finely chopped. Use the tamper to push the vegetables into the blades if necessary. Add the crab, lime zest and juice, cayenne pepper, coriander sprigs, Tabasco and mayonnaise and season with salt and pepper. Continue to pulse on and off a few times until the mixture forms a coarse paste. Do not over-process.
3 Transfer to a bowl and mix in enough of the breadcrumbs to form a stiff mixture. Put the remaining breadcrumbs on a plate. Wash the Vita-Mix machine.
4 Shape the crab mixture into 8 patties of equal size. Coat in the breadcrumbs, pressing the crumbs onto each side. Transfer to a clean plate, cover with cling film and chill for 30 minutes.
5 Put all the ingredients for the dipping sauce in the Vita-Mix machine and secure the 2-part lid. Select VARIABLE speed 2 and run for 5 seconds, then select HIGH and run for 1 minute until smooth. Pour the sauce into a bowl and set aside.
6 Heat the olive oil in a frying pan over a medium–high heat, then add half of the crab cakes and fry for 2 minutes on each side until crisp and golden. Transfer to a plate and keep warm while you cook the remaining cakes. Serve warm with the dipping sauce.

HEALTH BENEFITS • Energizing • Immune-boosting • Stress-busting • High protein • Low carb

Snacks
& Side Dishes

Marinated Green Beans

Lemon, Coriander & Green Olive Hummus

SERVES 4 **PREPARATION TIME:** 5 minutes, plus overnight soaking **VITA-MIX TIME:** 40 seconds
COOKING TIME: 1 hour 30 minutes **SERVE WITH:** Sesame Falafel (see page 73) and warm pitta bread
or crudités **STORAGE:** This can be kept in the fridge for up to 3 days.

200g/7oz dried chickpeas, soaked in water overnight • juice of 1 lemon • 3 tbsp extra-virgin olive oil
• 2–3 garlic cloves • 50g/1¾oz sesame seeds • 8 pitted green olives • 1 handful coriander leaves
• salt and freshly ground black pepper

1 Drain the chickpeas, put them in a pan and cover with water. Bring to the boil then reduce the heat to
   medium and simmer, covered, for 1½ hours or until soft. Drain.
2 Put the chickpeas, lemon juice, oil, garlic, sesame seeds and 170ml/5½fl oz water in the Vita-Mix machine,
   in that order, and secure the 2-part lid. Select VARIABLE speed 1. Turn the machine on and increase the
   speed to 10, then to HIGH. Run for 30 seconds or until smooth, using the tamper to push the ingredients
   into the blades. Add a little extra water if needed.
3 With the machine still running, remove the lid plug and add the olives and coriander and season with salt
   and pepper. Continue to run for 8–10 seconds or until finely chopped and well mixed, then serve.

HEALTH BENEFITS • Energizing • Immune-boosting • Anti-ageing • Stress-busting • High protein
• High fibre • Low carb • Low cholesterol • Low saturated fat

Guacamole

SERVES 4 **PREPARATION TIME:** 10 minutes **VITA-MIX TIME:** 28 seconds
STORAGE: Best served straight away, although it can be kept in the fridge until the following day.

2 large ripe avocados, halved and pitted • 2 tbsp lemon juice • 2 small tomatoes, halved • ½ shallot
• ½ red chilli, deseeded • 1 handful coriander • salt and freshly ground black pepper

1 Scoop the avocado flesh into the Vita-Mix machine, add the lemon juice and secure the 2-part lid. Select
VARIABLE speed 3 and run for 15–20 seconds or until the avocados are mashed.
2 With the machine still running, remove the lid plug, add the remaining ingredients and season with salt
and pepper. Run for 8 seconds, , using the tamper to push the ingredients into the blades if necessary
and taking care no to over-process – the mixture should be chunky. Serve immediately.

HEALTH BENEFITS • Energizing • Immune-boosting • Anti-ageing • Stress-busting • Weight-shifting
• High fibre • Low carb • Low cholesterol • Low saturated fat

Moroccan-Style Butterbean Dip

SERVES 4 **PREPARATION TIME:** 5 minutes **VITA-MIX TIME:** 1 minute **SERVE AS:** A dip or spread
on bread and crackers **STORAGE:** This can be kept in the fridge for up to 2 days.

400g/14oz tinned butterbeans, rinsed and drained • ¼ red pepper, deseeded • 3 dried ready-to-eat
apricots • 2 tbsp extra-virgin olive oil • 1 tbsp lemon juice • 1 garlic clove • 1 tsp smoked paprika
• ¼ tsp cumin • a pinch cayenne pepper • salt and freshly ground black pepper

1 Put the butterbeans and the remaining ingredients in the Vita-Mix machine with 55ml/1¾fl oz water
and secure the 2-part lid.
2 Select VARIABLE speed 6 and run for 1 minute or until well mixed, using the tamper to push the
ingredients into the blades, then serve.

HEALTH BENEFITS • Energizing • Detoxifying • Immune-boosting • Anti-ageing • Stress-busting
• Weight-shifting • High protein • High fibre • Low carb • Low cholesterol • Low saturated fat
• Low calorie • Low kilojoule

Tofu, Sweet Potato & Miso Spread

SERVES 4 **PREPARATION TIME:** 5 minutes, plus 1 hour chilling **VITA-MIX TIME:** 1 minute
COOKING TIME: 15 minutes **SERVE WITH:** Sourdough bread or rice cakes and a salad, or use
as a sandwich filling **STORAGE:** This can be kept in the fridge for up to 2 days.

1 sweet potato, peeled and diced • 375g/13oz plain tofu, diced • 3 tbsp extra-virgin olive oil
• 1 tbsp miso • 2 garlic cloves • 1 tsp tamari

1 Put the sweet potato in a steamer and cook for 15 minutes or until soft.
2 Transfer the sweet potato to the Vita-Mix machine, add the remaining ingredients and secure the 2-part
lid. Select VARIABLE speed 1. Turn the machine on and increase the speed to 10, then to HIGH. Run
for 1 minute or until smooth, using the tamper to push the ingredients into the blades.
3 Chill for 1 hour, then serve.

HEALTH BENEFITS • Energizing • Immune-boosting • Anti-ageing • Stress-busting • Weight-shifting
• High protein • High fibre • Low cholesterol • Low saturated fat • Low calorie • Low kilojoule

Sun-Dried Tomato & Black Olive Tapenade on Bruschetta

SERVES 4 **PREPARATION TIME:** 10 minutes **VITA-MIX TIME:** 30 seconds **COOKING TIME:** 4 minutes
STORAGE: The tapenade can be made in advance and kept in the fridge for up to 3 days.

Tapenade 200g/7oz pitted black olives • 8 sun-dried tomatoes, soaked in water • 1 garlic clove
• 2 basil sprigs • 6 tbsp extra-virgin olive oil • juice of ½ lemon • salt and freshly ground black pepper
Bruschetta 1 ciabatta • 1 tbsp extra-virgin olive oil • 1 garlic clove, crushed • 4 tomatoes, sliced

1 Preheat the grill to medium. Put the ingredients for the tapenade in the Vita-Mix machine, season with salt and pepper and secure the 2-part lid. Select VARIABLE speed 6 and run for 30 seconds or until well mixed, using the tamper to push the ingredients into the blades. Transfer to a bowl.
2 Slice the ciabatta in half horizontally and then lengthways. Brush with the oil and sprinkle with the garlic, then grill for 3–4 minutes until golden. Serve topped with the tapenade and tomatoes.

HEALTH BENEFITS • Energizing • Immune-boosting • Low cholesterol • Low saturated fat

Make this: *diabetic-friendly by using wholemeal bread instead of the ciabatta.*

Roasted Red Pepper Mousse

SERVES 4 **PREPARATION TIME:** 15 minutes, plus 5 hours chilling **VITA-MIX TIME:** 4 minutes
COOKING TIME: 15 minutes **SERVE WITH:** Rice cakes or melba toast and a watercress or spinach salad
STORAGE: This will keep in the fridge for up to 3 days.

4 red peppers, halved and deseeded • 1 tbsp powdered gelatine • 200g/7oz tomatoes
• 2 basil sprigs • a pinch cayenne pepper • a pinch sugar • 2 tsp balsamic vinegar • 2 egg whites
• freshly ground black pepper

1 Preheat the grill to high. Put the red peppers cut-side down on a baking sheet and grill for 15 minutes or until the skins blacken. Transfer to a bowl, cover with cling film and leave to cool. Once cool enough to handle, peel and discard the skins.
2 Put 2 tbsp cold water in a small bowl and sprinkle the gelatine over, then leave to stand for 5 minutes.
3 Put the red peppers, tomatoes, basil, cayenne pepper, sugar and vinegar in the Vita-Mix machine and secure the 2-part lid. Select VARIABLE speed 3. Turn the machine on and increase the speed to 10, then to HIGH. Run for 3 minutes until hot and steaming, then add the gelatine and run on HIGH for a further 1 minute until the gelatine has dissolved and is thoroughly combined. Strain the mixture through a sieve into a bowl and season with pepper.
4 In a clean bowl, whisk the egg whites until soft peaks form. Fold them into the pepper mixture and divide the mixture into four 150ml/5fl oz ramekins. Cover with cling film, chill for 5 hours until set, then serve.

HEALTH BENEFITS • Detoxifying • Immune-boosting • Anti-ageing • Stress-busting • Weight-shifting
• Low cholesterol • Low saturated fat • Low calorie • Low kilojoule

Make this: *vegetarian by using agar agar instead of gelatine; use 1 tablespoon agar agar powder or 3 tablespoons agar agar flakes and simmer in 90ml/3fl oz water until dissolved.*

Beetroot, Salmon & Mascarpone Pâté

SERVES 4 **PREPARATION TIME:** 5 minutes **VITA-MIX TIME:** 9 seconds **SERVE WITH:** Gluten-free or wholemeal bread and watercress **STORAGE:** This will keep in the fridge for up to 3 days.

1 dill sprig • 350g/12oz mascarpone cheese • 1 tbsp lemon juice • 75g/2½oz cooked baby beetroot, without vinegar • 150g/5½oz smoked salmon • freshly ground black pepper

1 Put the dill, mascarpone and lemon juice in the Vita-Mix machine and secure the 2-part lid. Select VARIABLE speed 3 and run for 3–4 seconds until the dill is chopped. Switch off the machine. Add the beetroot and salmon. Select VARIABLE speed 1. Turn the machine on and increase the speed to 5, using the tamper to press the beetroot and salmon into the blades. Run for 4–5 seconds until coarsely chopped and combined. Do not over-process.
2 Transfer to a bowl and season with pepper. Cover and chill until ready to serve.

HEALTH BENEFITS • Immune-boosting • Energizing • Anti-ageing • Stress-busting • High protein

Red Lentil Dal

SERVES 4 **PREPARATION TIME:** 10 minutes **VITA-MIX TIME:** 30 seconds
COOKING TIME: 20 minutes **SERVE WITH:** Warm naan bread
STORAGE: Best served straight away, although it can be kept in the fridge until the following day.

200g/7oz red lentils • 1 tomato, halved • 2 garlic cloves • 1 carrot, peeled and quartered
• 2cm/¾in piece root ginger, peeled • ¼ green chilli, deseeded • 1 tsp cumin • ½ tsp mustard seeds
• a pinch turmeric • 60ml/2fl oz coconut milk • 1 tsp olive oil • 1 tbsp lemon juice • salt and freshly
ground black pepper

1 Put the lentils in a saucepan and cover with 500ml/17fl oz water. Bring to the boil over a high heat,
then reduce the heat to medium-low and simmer, covered, for 20 minutes, stirring occasionally.
2 Transfer the lentils to the Vita-Mix machine and add the remaining ingredients in the order listed. Season
with salt and pepper and secure the 2-part lid. Turn the machine on and increase the speed to 10, then
to HIGH. Run for 30 seconds or until smooth, using the tamper to push the ingredients into the blades.
Serve immediately.

HEALTH BENEFITS • Energizing • Detoxifying • Immune-boosting • Anti-ageing • Stress-busting
• Weight-shifting • High protein • High fibre • Low carb • Low cholesterol • Low saturated fat
• Low calorie • Low kilojoule

Make this: *citrus-free by omitting the lemon juice. Make this nut-free by omitting the coconut milk.*

Refried Beans

SERVES 4 **PREPARATION TIME:** 5 minutes, plus overnight soaking
VITA-MIX TIME: 5–10 seconds **COOKING TIME:** 1 hour
SERVE WITH: A spicy rice dish or in wheat tortillas with Guacamole (see page 85), soured cream
and grated cheese **STORAGE:** This can be kept in the fridge until the following day.

250g/9oz dried pinto beans, soaked in water overnight • 2 tbsp olive oil • 2 garlic cloves
• 1cm/½in piece red chilli, deseeded • 1 tsp ground cumin • a pinch cayenne pepper
• ½ tsp chilli powder • 1 tbsp tamari • salt and freshly ground black pepper

1 Drain the beans, put them in a large saucepan and cover with water. Bring to the boil over a high heat,
then reduce the heat to medium-low and simmer, covered, for 1 hour or until soft. Drain well.
2 Heat the oil in a pan over a medium heat. Add the beans and cook for 2 minutes, stirring occasionally.
3 Put the garlic, red chilli, beans, cumin, cayenne pepper, chilli powder, 4 tablespoons water and tamari,
in that order in the Vita-Mix machine. Season with salt and pepper and secure the 2-part lid. Select
VARIABLE speed 1 and pulse on and off several times until the beans start to purée, using the tamper
to push them into the blades. Do not over-process. Serve immediately.

HEALTH BENEFITS • Energizing • Immune-boosting • Anti-ageing • Stress-busting • Weight-shifting
• High protein • High fibre • Low carb • Low cholesterol • Low saturated fat • Low calorie
• Low kilojoule

Sweet Potato, Artichoke & Carrot Mash

SERVES 4 **PREPARATION TIME:** 10 minutes **VITA-MIX TIME:** 1 minute 5 seconds
COOKING TIME: 20 minutes **SERVE WITH:** Marinated Seared Steaks with Sweet Onion Chutney
(see page 132) and a leafy green salad **STORAGE:** Best served straight away.

850g/1lb 14oz sweet potatoes, peeled and diced • 625g/1lb 6oz carrots, peeled and chopped
• 390g/13¾oz tinned artichoke hearts, drained • 4 tbsp crème fraîche • 1 handful flat-leaf parsley
(optional) • salt and freshly ground black pepper

1 Put the sweet potatoes and carrots in a steamer and cook for 20 minutes or until soft, then transfer
   to the Vita-Mix machine.
2 Add the artichokes and crème fraîche and season with salt and pepper, then secure the 2-part lid.
   Select VARIABLE speed 3 and run for 1 minute or until the vegetables are creamy, using the tamper
   to push them into the blades.
3 With the machine still running, remove the lid plug and add the parsley, if using. Run for 5 seconds
   or until finely chopped and well mixed, then serve.

HEALTH BENEFITS • Energizing • Immune-boosting • Anti-ageing • Stress-busting • High fibre
• Low cholesterol • Low saturated fat

Make this: *vegan and dairy-free by using 1 tablespoon olive oil instead of crème fraîche.*

Root Vegetable & Horseradish Mash

SERVES 4 **PREPARATION TIME:** 15 minutes **VITA-MIX TIME:** 1 minute
COOKING TIME: 25 minutes **SERVE WITH:** Baked chicken or grilled tofu
STORAGE: Best served straight away **IF USING THE 32oz CONTAINER:** Halve the quantities.

700g/1lb 9oz floury potatoes, peeled and diced • 200g/7oz parsnips, peeled and chopped
• 200g/7oz carrots, peeled and chopped • 100g/3½oz swede, peeled and chopped (optional)
• 10g/¼oz horseradish, peeled • 55ml/1¾fl oz full-fat milk • 2 tsp olive oil • salt and freshly
ground black pepper

1 Put the potatoes, parsnips, carrots and swede, if using, in a steamer and cook for 20–25 minutes until soft.
2 Transfer the vegetables to the Vita-Mix machine and add the remaining ingredients. Season with salt and
   pepper and secure the 2-part lid. Select VARIABLE speed 3. Run for 1 minute or until the vegetables are
   creamy, using the tamper to push them into the blades, then serve.

HEALTH BENEFITS • Energizing • Immune-boosting • Stress-busting • High fibre • Low cholesterol
• Low saturated fat

Make this: *vegan and dairy-free by using soya milk instead of full-fat milk.*

Herb Mash

SERVES 4 **PREPARATION TIME:** 10 minutes **VITA-MIX TIME:** 20 seconds
COOKING TIME: 17 minutes **STORAGE:** Best served straight away.
IF USING THE 32oz CONTAINER: Halve the quantities.

1.5 kg/3lb 5oz floury potatoes, peeled and diced • 2 thyme sprigs • 2 rosemary sprigs
• 80ml/2½fl oz full-fat milk • 3 tbsp soured cream • ½ tsp butter • 1 handful flat-leaf parsley
• 12 chives • 5 sage leaves • salt and freshly ground black pepper

1 Bring a large saucepan of water to the boil and add the potatoes, thyme and rosemary. Reduce the heat
  to medium and simmer, covered, for 10–15 minutes or until tender. Drain and discard the herbs.
2 Warm the milk in a saucepan over a low heat.
3 Put the potatoes, milk, soured cream and butter in the Vita-Mix machine and season with salt and pepper.
  Secure the 2-part lid, select VARIABLE speed 3 and run for 15 seconds or until creamy, using the tamper
  to push them into the blades. With the machine still running, remove the lid plug and add the parsley,
  chives and sage. Run for 5 seconds or until they are finely chopped, then serve.

HEALTH BENEFITS • Energizing

Braised Red Cabbage
with Onions & Apples

SERVES 4 **PREPARATION TIME:** 10 minutes **VITA-MIX TIME:** 30 seconds
COOKING TIME: 30 minutes **SERVE WITH:** Stuffed Roasted Quail with Wild Mushroom Cream
(see page 163) **STORAGE:** Best served straight away.

55ml/1¾fl oz vegetable stock • 3 tbsp red wine vinegar • 1 garlic clove • 2.5cm/1in piece root ginger,
peeled • 1 tbsp demerara sugar • 1 red cabbage, quartered • 2 red onions, halved • 2 apples, cored
and chopped • 1 tbsp sunflower oil • 1 bay leaf • 2 thyme sprigs • salt and freshly ground black pepper

1 Preheat the oven to 190°C/375°F/Gas 5. Put the vegetable stock, vinegar, garlic, ginger and sugar
   in the Vita-Mix machine and secure the 2-part lid. Select VARIABLE speed 1. Turn the machine on and
   increase the speed to 10, then to HIGH. Run for 10 seconds until well mixed, then transfer to a bowl.
   Wash the Vita-Mix machine.
2 Put some of the cabbage in the Vita-Mix machine and secure the 2-part lid. Select VARIABLE speed 1
   and run for 4–5 seconds until chopped, using the tamper to push the cabbage into the blades if necessary.
   Transfer to a large bowl and repeat the process until all the cabbage has been chopped.
3 Repeat the same chopping process for the onions and add them and the apples to the cabbage.
4 Heat the oil in a large pan over a medium-high heat. Add the cabbage, onions and apples and cook
   for 3 minutes, stirring frequently, until the mixture begins to soften. Transfer the mixture to a lidded
   casserole dish and add the stock mixture, bay leaf and thyme. Season with salt and pepper and bake
   for 20–25 minutes or until most of the liquid has evaporated. Serve hot.

HEALTH BENEFITS • Energizing • Detoxifying • Immune-boosting • Anti-ageing • Stress-busting
• Weight-shifting • High fibre • Low cholesterol • Low saturated fat • Low calorie • Low kilojoule

Fennel Coleslaw in Tofu Dressing

SERVES 4 **PREPARATION TIME:** 10 minutes **VITA-MIX TIME:** 1 minute
STORAGE: Best served straight away. The dressing can be made in advance and kept in the fridge for up to 2 days.

1 fennel bulb, quartered • 125g/4½oz white cabbage • 2 carrots, peeled and quartered
• 1 spring onion, chopped
Dressing 150g/5½oz tofu, diced • 3 tbsp olive oil • 1–2 tbsp lemon juice • 1 tsp mustard powder
• 1 tsp clear honey • salt and freshly ground black pepper

1 Put the fennel in the Vita-Mix machine and secure the 2-part lid. Select VARIABLE speed 1. Turn the machine on and run for 3–4 seconds until finely chopped. Transfer to a salad bowl and repeat the process for the cabbage and carrots, using the tamper to push the vegetables into the blades, if necessary. Add the spring onion to the salad and toss.
2 Put the ingredients for the dressing in the Vita-Mix machine and add 70ml/2¼fl oz water. Secure the 2-part lid and select VARIABLE speed 1. Turn the machine on and increase the speed to 10, then to HIGH. Run for 45 seconds or until smooth and creamy. Pour the dressing over the salad, toss well and serve.

HEALTH BENEFITS •Energizing • Detoxifying • Immune-boosting • Anti-ageing • Stress-busting
• Weight-shifting • High fibre • Low carb • Low cholesterol • Low saturated fat • Low calorie
• Low kilojoule

Marinated Green Beans

SERVES 4 **PREPARATION TIME:** 5 minutes, plus 1 hour marinating
VITA-MIX TIME: 35 seconds **COOKING TIME:** 2 minutes
SERVE WITH: Chorizo & Feta-Stuffed Chicken (see page 117) or Vegetarian Moussaka (see page 154)
STORAGE: Best served on the same day.

400g/14oz extra-fine green beans, trimmed • 1 tomato, halved • 2.5cm/1in piece red chilli, deseeded
• ½ garlic clove • 125ml/4fl oz olive oil • 1 tbsp lemon juice • 1 tsp clear honey • 3 flat-leaf parsley sprigs
• 3 coriander sprigs • freshly ground black pepper

1 Bring a pan of water to the boil and add the green beans. Bring back to the boil and cook for 2 minutes, then drain. The beans should be crisp. Transfer to a large bowl.
2 Meanwhile, put the tomato, chilli, garlic, oil, lemon juice and honey in the Vita-Mix machine and season with pepper. Secure the 2-part lid and select VARIABLE speed 1. Turn the machine on and increase the speed to 10, then to HIGH. Run for 30 seconds until smooth.
3 Remove the lid plug, add the parsley and coriander and pulse on and off a few times until finely chopped.
4 Pour the marinade over the green beans and leave to marinate at room temperature for 1 hour, then serve.

HEALTH BENEFITS • Energizing • Detoxifying • Immune-boosting • Anti-ageing • Stress-busting
• Weight-shifting • High fibre • Low carb • Low cholesterol • Low saturated fat • Low calorie
• Low kilojoule

Make this: vegan by using brown rice syrup instead of honey.

Steamed Asparagus with Béarnaise Sauce

SERVES 4 **PREPARATION TIME:** 5 minutes **VITA-MIX TIME:** 2 minutes 20 seconds
COOKING TIME: 4 minutes **SERVE WITH:** Scrambled Eggs (see page 58) or grilled meat or fish
STORAGE: Leftovers will keep in the fridge until the following day.

20 asparagus spears, trimmed
Sauce 6 egg yolks • 1 tarragon sprig • 3 tbsp white wine vinegar • 1 tbsp white wine
• 200g/7oz butter, melted • 1 tsp lemon juice • salt and freshly ground black pepper

1 Put the asparagus in a steamer and cook for 3–4 minutes until just tender, then transfer to a plate.
2 While the asparagus is cooking, put the egg yolks and tarragon in the Vita-Mix machine and secure the 2-part lid. Select VARIABLE speed 1. Turn the machine on and increase the speed to 3. Run for 20 seconds until well mixed.
3 Remove the lid plug and, with the machine still running, slowly pour the vinegar and wine into the Vita-Mix machine, followed by the melted butter and run for 2 minutes until the sauce is creamy and pale. Add the lemon juice to taste, and season with salt and pepper.
4 Spoon the sauce over the asparagus and serve immediately.

HEALTH BENEFITS • Energizing • Stress-busting • High protein • Low carb

Ratatouille

SERVES 4 **PREPARATION TIME:** 15 minutes **VITA-MIX TIME:** 35 seconds
COOKING TIME: 40 minutes **SERVE WITH:** Brown rice and a leafy green salad
STORAGE: The sauce can be made in advance and kept in the fridge until the following day.

700g/1lb 9oz tomatoes, halved • 4 tbsp olive oil • 4 tbsp tomato purée • ½ small onion • 3 garlic cloves • 1 tsp paprika • 1 handful flat-leaf parsley • 1 tsp dried mixed herbs • 2 red onions, chopped • 1 red pepper, deseeded and chopped • 1 yellow pepper, deseeded and chopped • 2 courgettes, trimmed and chopped • 1 aubergine, diced • salt and freshly ground black pepper

1 Preheat the oven to 200°C/400°F/Gas 6. Put the tomatoes cut-side up in a baking dish. Add 2 tablespoons of the oil and mix well. Bake for 15–20 minutes until tender, stirring occasionally.
2 Transfer the tomatoes to the Vita-Mix machine and add the tomato purée, onion, garlic and paprika. Secure the 2-part lid and select VARIABLE speed 1. Turn the machine on and increase the speed to 10, then to HIGH. Run for 30 seconds or until smooth.
3 With the machine still running, remove the lid plug, add the parsley and mixed herbs and season with salt and pepper. Run for a further 5 seconds until well mixed, then set aside.
4 Heat the remaining oil in a large saucepan over a medium heat. Add the red onions and lightly fry for 4–5 minutes, stirring occasionally, until beginning to soften. Add the peppers and courgettes and cook for a further 6 minutes until softened, then add the aubergine. Cook for 8 minutes, stirring occasionally, until cooked through.
5 Stir the tomato sauce into the vegetables and heat through, then serve.

HEALTH BENEFITS • Energizing • Detoxifying • Immune-boosting • Anti-ageing • Stress-busting • Weight-shifting • High fibre • Low carb • Low cholesterol • Low saturated fat • Low calorie • Low kilojoule

Gado-Gado

SERVES 4 **PREPARATION TIME:** 5 minutes **VITA-MIX TIME:** 1 minute
COOKING TIME: 5 minutes **SERVE WITH:** Brown rice or rice noodles
STORAGE: Best served straight away, although the sauce can be made in advance and kept in the fridge for up to 2 days.

1–2 tbsp sesame oil • 200g/7oz baby carrots, cut into matchsticks • 8 baby corn, chopped
• 2 pak choi, chopped • 300g/10½oz bean sprouts
Peanut Sauce 125g/4½oz roasted unsalted peanuts • 1 tbsp soy sauce • juice of ½ lime
• 2 tbsp vegetable oil • 1 garlic clove • ½ tsp chilli powder • 1 tsp sugar • salt

1 Put the ingredients for the sauce in the Vita-Mix machine and season with salt. Add 150ml/5fl oz water and secure the 2-part lid. Select VARIABLE speed 1. Turn the machine on and increase the speed to 10, then to HIGH. Run for 1 minute or until smooth, using the tamper to push the ingredients into the blades if necessary, then set aside.
2 Heat the sesame oil in a large frying pan or wok over a high heat. Add the carrots, baby corn and pak choi and stir-fry for 3 minutes until beginning to soften. Add the bean sprouts and continue stir-frying for a further 2 minutes until tender. Serve immediately with the peanut sauce.

HEALTH BENEFITS • Energizing • Weight-shifting • High protein • High fibre • Low carb
• Low cholesterol • Low saturated fat • Low calorie • Low kilojoule

Spinach, Pear & Almond Salad with Herby Roquefort Dressing

SERVES 4 **PREPARATION TIME:** 10 minutes **VITA-MIX TIME:** 35 seconds
SERVE WITH: Grilled fish or meat **STORAGE:** Best served straight away. The dressing can be made in advance and kept in an airtight container in the fridge for up to 1 day.

150g/5½oz baby spinach leaves • 2 firm pears, cored and chopped • 50g/1¾oz almonds
Dressing 4 tbsp mayonnaise • 4 tbsp soured cream • 1 tsp lemon juice • 55g/2oz Roquefort cheese, crumbled • ½ garlic clove • 1–2 basil leaves (optional) • salt and freshly ground black pepper

1 Put the spinach and pears in a large salad bowl.
2 Put the almonds in the Vita-Mix machine and secure the 2-part lid. Select VARIABLE speed 1 and pulse on and off several times until the nuts are chopped, then add them to the salad bowl.
3 Put the ingredients for the dressing in the Vita-Mix machine and season with salt and pepper. Secure the 2-part lid and select VARIABLE speed 6. Run for 30 seconds or until smooth and creamy. Pour the dressing over the salad, toss well and serve.

HEALTH BENEFITS • Energizing • Immune-boosting • Anti-ageing • High protein • Low carb

Luxury Waldorf Salad with Garlic Mayonnaise

SERVES 4 **PREPARATION TIME:** 10 minutes **VITA-MIX TIME:** 20 seconds
SERVE WITH: Tomato Pesto & Black Olive Pizza (see page 74) or grilled meat or fish
STORAGE: Best served straight away. The dressing can be made in advance and kept in the fridge for up to 2 days. The extra garlic mayonnaise can be kept in the fridge for up to 2 days.

125g/4½oz mixed salad leaves, such as rocket, watercress and lettuce • 2 celery sticks, chopped • 1 red apple, cored and chopped • 100g/3½oz white seedless grapes, halved • 60g/2¼oz chopped walnuts
Mayonnaise 1 egg • 1 egg yolk • 1 tbsp lemon juice • ½ tsp Dijon mustard • 1 small garlic clove
• 125ml/4fl oz sunflower oil • 125ml/4fl oz olive oil • salt and freshly ground black pepper

1 Put the salad leaves, celery, apple, grapes and walnuts in a large salad bowl. Toss well and set aside.
2 To make the mayonnaise, put the egg, egg yolk, lemon juice, mustard, garlic and 1 tablespoon of the oil in the Vita-Mix machine. Season with salt and pepper and secure the 2-part lid. Select VARIABLE speed 5 and run for 10 seconds or until creamy.
3 With the machine still running, remove the lid plug and add the remaining sunflower and olive oil in a slow steady stream and continue to blend for a further 10 seconds or until thick. Pour the mayonnaise over the salad, toss well and serve immediately.

HEALTH BENEFITS • Energizing • Immune-boosting • Anti-ageing • High fibre • Low carb

Raw Beetroot, Carrot & Sunflower Seed Salad

SERVES 4 **PREPARATION TIME:** 10 minutes **VITA-MIX TIME:** 1 minute **COOKING TIME:** 3 minutes
SERVE WITH: Asparagus Tofu Quiche (see page 72) or Lebanese Lamb Pastries (See page 80)
STORAGE: Best served straight away. The dressing can be made in advance and kept in the fridge for up to 2 days.

3 beetroot, peeled and quartered • 3 carrots, peeled and quartered • 2 tbsp sunflower seeds
Dressing 50g/1¾oz sesame seeds • 1 tbsp lemon juice • a pinch mustard powder • a pinch paprika
• 1 handful flat-leaf parsley • salt and freshly ground black pepper

1 Put the beetroot in the Vita-Mix machine and secure the 2-part lid. Select VARIABLE speed 1. Turn the machine on and run for 3–4 seconds until finely chopped, using the tamper to help push the vegetables into the blades if necessary. Transfer to a salad bowl, then repeat with the carrots, adding them to the bowl once they are chopped. Add the sunflower seeds to the beetroot and carrots and mix well.
2 To make the dressing, put the sesame seeds in a dry heavy-based frying pan and cook for 3 minutes, stirring frequently, until lightly toasted.
3 Transfer the toasted sesame seeds to the Vita-Mix machine and add 100ml/3½oz water, the lemon juice, mustard powder and paprika. Season with salt and pepper and secure the 2-part lid. Select VARIABLE speed 1. Turn the machine on and increase the speed to 10, then to HIGH. Run for 45 seconds or until smooth and creamy. Remove the lid plug and add the parsley, then pulse on and off a few times until finely chopped. Pour the dressing over the salad, toss well and serve immediately.

HEALTH BENEFITS • Energizing • Detoxifying • Immune-boosting • Anti-ageing • Stress-busting
• Weight-shifting • High fibre • Low carb • Low cholesterol • Low saturated fat • Low calorie
• Low kilojoule

Dinners

Tagliatelle with Pumpkin Seed Pesto & Roasted Vegetables

Tofu & Spinach-Stuffed Aubergines

SERVES 4 **PREPARATION TIME:** 15 minutes **VITA-MIX TIME:** 1 minute 5 seconds
COOKING TIME: 1 hour 20 minutes **SERVE WITH:** Millet or quinoa
STORAGE: Best served straight away, although will keep in the fridge for up to 1 day.
IF USING THE 32oz CONTAINER: Halve the quantities.

2 large aubergines, trimmed and cut in half lengthways • 500g/1lb 2oz firm tofu, diced
• 125ml/4fl oz vegetable stock • 2 tbsp sunflower oil • small piece onion • 2 garlic cloves
• 1 tsp paprika • a pinch cayenne pepper • a pinch nutmeg • 1 tbsp lemon juice • 1 tbsp olive oil
• 100g/3½oz spinach leaves • salt and freshly ground black pepper

1   Preheat the oven to 190°C/375°F/Gas 5. Put the aubergines in a baking tray cut-side up and cover with foil. Bake for 30 minutes until soft, then leave to cool. When cool, scoop out the flesh and set it aside for use in another recipe. Return the aubergine shells to the baking tray.
2   Meanwhile, put all the remaining ingredients, except the spinach and oil, in the Vita-Mix machine and season with salt and pepper. Secure the 2-part lid and select VARIABLE speed 1. Turn the machine on and increase the speed to 10, then to HIGH. Run for 1 minute or until smooth, using the tamper to push the ingredients into the blades.
3   Heat the oil in a pan over a medium-high heat. Add the spinach and stir-fry for 1–2 minutes until wilted. Squeeze out any excess liquid, then add the spinach to the tofu mixture and secure the 2-part lid. Select VARIABLE speed 1 and pulse on and off a couple of times to chop the spinach, then stir the mixture to evenly distribute the spinach.
4   Spoon the tofu mixture into the aubergine shells and bake for 45 minutes or until set. Serve hot.

HEALTH BENEFITS • Energizing • Immune-boosting • Anti-ageing • Stress-busting
• Weight-shifting • High protein • High fibre • Low carb • Low cholesterol • Low saturated fat
• Low calorie • Low kilojoule

Make this: citrus-free by omitting the lemon juice.

Tofu & Potato Galette

SERVES 4–6 **PREPARATION TIME:** 15 minutes **VITA-MIX TIME:** 1 minute 20 seconds
COOKING TIME: 1 hour 40 minutes **SERVE WITH:** A tomato salad **STORAGE:** Leftovers will keep
in the fridge for up to 2 days. **NOT SUITABLE FOR THE 32oz CONTAINER.**

2 tbsp sunflower oil, plus extra for greasing • 550g/1lb 4oz potatoes • 50g/1¾oz cashew nuts
• 100ml/3½fl oz vegetable stock • 500g/1lb 2oz firm tofu, diced • 1 red pepper, quartered and deseeded
• ¼ red onion • 1 garlic clove • 1 tbsp lemon juice • 3 dill sprigs • salt and freshly ground black pepper

1   Preheat the oven to 180°C/350°F/Gas 4. Grease a 23cm/9in round baking dish with oil and set aside.
2   Bring a large pan of water to the boil and add the potatoes. Boil for 20 minutes or until just tender. Drain and set aside.
3   Meanwhile, put the remaining ingredients, except the dill, in the Vita-Mix machine and season with salt and pepper. Secure the 2-part lid. Select VARIABLE speed 1. Turn the machine on and increase the speed to 10, then to HIGH. Run for 1 minute or until smooth, using the tamper to push the ingredients into the blades. Remove the lid plug and add the dill. Replace the plug and pulse on and off until finely chopped.
4   Slice the potatoes and layer half of them in the baking dish. Spoon the tofu mixture on top and cover with a second layer of potatoes. Cover with foil and bake for 50 minutes, then remove the foil and bake for a further 30 minutes. Serve warm.

HEALTH BENEFITS • Energizing • Immune-boosting • Anti-ageing • Stress-busting • Weight-shifting
• High protein • High fibre • Low cholesterol • Low saturated fat • Low calorie • Low kilojoule

Make this: seed-free by using olive oil instead of sunflower oil.

Chilli Tofu Udon Bowl

SERVES 4 **PREPARATION TIME:** 15 minutes, plus at least 5 hours marinating
VITA-MIX TIME: 1 minute **COOKING TIME:** 25 minutes **SERVE WITH:** Stir-fried pak choi
STORAGE: Leftovers will keep in the fridge for up to 1 day. The sauce can be made in advance
and kept in the fridge for up to 2 days.

400g/14oz firm tofu, drained, patted dry and diced • 400g/14oz udon noodles • 2 tbsp sesame oil
• 1 tbsp sesame seeds
Marinade 4 tbsp soy sauce • juice of ½ lime • 1 tbsp sesame oil • ½ tsp toasted sesame oil
• 1 garlic clove • 2cm/¾in piece root ginger, peeled • 1 tsp clear honey
Sauce 8 tomatoes, halved • 2 tbsp tomato purée • 1 red pepper, quartered and deseeded
• ½ small shallot • 1 garlic clove • ¼ green chilli, deseeded • 2.5cm/1in piece lemongrass stalk,
peeled • a pinch red chilli flakes • a pinch brown sugar • salt

1 Put the ingredients for the marinade in the Vita-Mix machine and secure the 2-part lid. Select VARIABLE
  speed 1. Turn the machine on and increase the speed to 10, then to HIGH. Run for 30 seconds or until
  smooth. Put the tofu in a large bowl, pour the marinade over and mix well to coat. Cover and leave
  to marinate in the fridge for 5 hours or overnight.
2 To make the sauce, preheat the grill to medium. Put the tomatoes on a baking sheet and grill for
  7 minutes until softened. Transfer to the Vita-Mix machine and add the remaining ingredients for the
  sauce and season with salt. Secure the 2-part lid and select VARIABLE speed 1. Turn the machine on
  and increase the speed to 10, then to HIGH. Run for 30 seconds or until thoroughly mixed. Set aside.
3 Cook the udon noodles according to the packet instructions or until al dente. Rinse, drain and transfer
  to a saucepan.
4 Meanwhile, heat the sesame oil in a frying pan or wok over a medium heat and stir-fry the tofu for
  6 minutes until evenly browned. Add the sesame seeds and cook for a further 1 minute.
5 Add the sauce to the noodles, mix well and heat over a medium heat for 1–2 minutes until warmed
  through. Divide the noodles into four bowls, top with the tofu and serve.

HEALTH BENEFITS • Energizing • Immune-boosting • Stress-busting • High protein • Low cholesterol
• Low saturated fat

Baked Cod with Bacon
& Herb Crust

SERVES 4 **PREPARATION TIME:** 10 minutes **VITA-MIX TIME:** 10 seconds
COOKING TIME: 10 minutes **SERVE WITH:** Steamed vegetables and new or mashed potatoes
STORAGE: The bacon crust can be made up to 2 days in advance. Cover and chill in the fridge
until ready to use. Leftovers will keep in the fridge until the following day.

50g/1¾oz bread, about 2 slices • 4 flat-leaf parsley sprigs • 2 streaky bacon rashers
• juice and zest of 1 lemon • 25g/1oz butter • 4 cod fillets, about 125g/4½oz each
• 1 tbsp olive oil, plus extra for greasing

1 Preheat the oven to 200°C/400°F/Gas 6 and lightly grease a baking dish. To make the crust, secure
  the 2-part lid on the Vita-Mix and select VARIABLE speed 2. Turn the machine on and, with the lid plug
  removed, feed the bread and parsley into the container, using the tamper to push them into the blades.
  Run for 5 seconds until fine breadcrumbs form. Transfer to a bowl and set aside.
2 Put the bacon, lemon zest and butter in the Vita-Mix machine and secure the 2-part lid. Select
  VARIABLE speed 2 and pulse on and off a few times until the bacon is finely chopped and mixed into
  the butter. Add the bacon butter to the breadcrumbs and mix thoroughly until the mixture forms a paste.
3 Put the fish fillets in the baking dish and sprinkle the lemon juice over. Spread the bacon crust over the
  top of each fillet and press down gently, then drizzle with the oil.
4 Bake for 10 minutes until cooked through and the topping is golden brown, then serve.

HEALTH BENEFITS • Energizing • Stress-busting • High protein • Low carb

Tagliatelle with Flaked Salmon & Béchamel Sauce

SERVES 4 **PREPARATION TIME:** 10 minutes **VITA-MIX TIME:** 5 minutes **COOKING TIME:** 10 minutes
SERVE WITH: A leafy green salad **STORAGE:** Leftovers will keep in the fridge for up to 2 days.

400g/14oz tagliatelle • 60g/2¼oz pine nuts • 300g/10½oz hot-smoked salmon, skinned and
flaked into chunks • 60g/2¼oz rocket leaves or watercress • 2 tbsp grated Parmesan cheese
• freshly ground black pepper
Sauce 300ml/10½fl oz full-fat or semi-skimmed milk • 40g/1½oz plain flour • 40g/1½oz butter
• 1 tbsp lemon juice

1 Bring a large pan of water to the boil and cook the tagliatelle according to the packet instructions until
al dente. Drain and return to the pan.
2 While the pasta is cooking, put the pine nuts in a heavy-based saucepan over a medium heat and toast,
stirring continuously, for 2–3 minutes until lightly browned, then transfer to a plate and set aside.
3 Put the milk in a pan and heat over a medium heat until warm. Transfer to the Vita-Mix machine and
add the remaining ingredients for the sauce in the order listed. Secure the 2-part lid and select VARIABLE
speed 1. Turn the machine on and increase the speed to 10, then to HIGH. Run for 5 minutes until thick
and steaming. Pour the sauce over the pasta, then add the salmon, rocket and pine nuts.
4 Stir over a low heat for 1 minute until the rocket leaves have wilted. Season with pepper and serve
immediately sprinkled with the Parmesan cheese.

Health Benefits • Energizing • Stress-busting • High protein

Seafood Pie

SERVES 4–6 **PREPARATION TIME:** 15 minutes **VITA-MIX TIME:** 5 minutes 11 seconds
COOKING TIME: 55 minutes **SERVE WITH:** Steamed green vegetables **STORAGE:** Prepare in advance
and chill, uncooked, for up to 1 day. It can also be frozen, uncooked, for up to 1 month. Defrost in the
fridge overnight before cooking. Leftovers will keep in the fridge for up to 1 day.
IF USING THE 32oz CONTAINER: Halve the quantities.

1kg/2lb 4oz floury potatoes, peeled and cut into chunks • 100g/3½oz Cheddar cheese • 2 shallots
• 70ml/2¼fl oz white wine • 150ml/5fl oz double cream • 2 tsp cornflour • 200ml/7fl oz full-fat milk
• a pinch saffron strands • 1 tbsp olive oil • 350g/12oz smoked haddock fillets, skinned and cut into
chunks • 350g/12oz white fish fillets, skinned and cut into chunks • 150g/5½oz raw, peeled prawns
• 150g/5½oz white crabmeat

1 Heat the oven to 200°C/400°F/Gas 6. Bring a large pan of salted water to the boil. Add the potatoes,
then reduce the heat to medium-low and simmer for 15 minutes or until tender, then drain.
2 While the potatoes are cooking, put the cheese in the Vita-Mix machine and secure the 2-part lid.
Select VARIABLE speed 3 and run for 3–4 seconds until finely chopped. Transfer to a bowl and set aside.
3 Put the shallots, white wine, cream and cornflour in the Vita-Mix machine and secure the 2-part lid. Select
VARIABLE speed 1. Turn the machine on and increase the speed to 10, then to HIGH. Run for 4–5 minutes
until hot and thick. Transfer to a bowl and leave to cool slightly. Wash the Vita-Mix machine.
4 Put the milk in a pan and heat over a medium heat for 2 minutes, stirring occasionally, until hot. Transfer
the milk to the Vita-Mix machine and add the saffron, oil and potatoes. Secure the 2-part lid and select
VARIABLE speed 1. Turn the machine on and increase the speed to 6, using the tamper to press the
potatoes into the blades. Run for 6–7 seconds until the mixture forms a smooth mash.
5 Mix together the sauce, fish and prawns and put in a shallow baking dish. Scatter over the crabmeat, top
with the potato and sprinkle with the cheese. Bake for 30–40 minutes until golden brown, then serve.

HEALTH BENEFITS • Energizing • Stress-busting • High protein

Make this: *sugar-free by using fish stock instead of wine. Make this dairy-free by omitting the cheese
and using soya cream and soya milk instead of double cream and full-fat milk.*

Salmon & Dill Cream Ravioli

SERVES 4 **PREPARATION TIME:** 20 minutes, plus 20 minutes resting **VITA-MIX TIME:** 8 seconds
COOKING TIME: 20 minutes **SERVE WITH:** A leafy green salad **STORAGE:** Leftovers will keep
in the fridge for up to 2 days. **IF USING THE 32oz CONTAINER:** Halve the quantities.

Pasta dough 300g/10½oz '00' flour or strong white bread flour, plus extra for rolling the dough
• 4 large eggs • semolina, for kneading
Filling 500g/1lb 2oz salmon fillet, skinned and cut into chunks • 2 dill sprigs, plus extra, to serve
• 80ml/2½fl oz double cream • 1 tbsp lemon juice • freshly ground black pepper • 3 tbsp olive oil,
plus extra to serve

1 To make the dough, put the flour in a large bowl. Make a well in the centre and add 3 of the eggs. Whisk
the eggs together with a fork, then gradually stir in the flour to form a soft dough. Lightly dust a work
surface with semolina and knead the dough until smooth, then roll it into a ball and wrap in cling film.
Leave to rest for 20 minutes at room temperature.
2 To make the filling, put the salmon and dill in the Vita-Mix machine. Secure the 2-part lid, select VARIABLE
speed 1 and pulse on and off for 3–4 seconds until the mixture forms a paste. With the machine still
running, add the cream. Run for 3–4 seconds until smooth. Stir in the lemon juice and season with pepper.
3 On a well-floured surface, roll the dough out thinly. Cut out 40 rounds using a 4cm/1½in pastry cutter.
Put 1 teaspoon of the filling in the centre of half the circles. Beat the remaining egg and lightly brush
the edges of the circles. Cover with the remaining circles and press the edges together to seal.
4 Bring a large pot of salted water to the boil. Add 1 tablespoon of the oil, then, working in batches, drop
in the ravioli and cook for 3–4 minutes. Remove with a slotted spoon and drain. Drizzle with the remaining
oil and serve immediately with the extra dill.

HEALTH BENEFITS • Energizing • Stress-busting • High protein

Pan-Fried Sea Bass
with Sorrel & Garlic Sauce

SERVES 4 **PREPARATION TIME:** 5 minutes **VITA-MIX TIME:** 4 minutes **COOKING TIME:** 4 minutes
SERVE WITH: Herb Mash (see page 91) and steamed leafy greens **STORAGE:** The sauce can be prepared
in advance and kept in the fridge for 2 days. Leftovers will keep in the fridge until the next day.

4 sea bass fillets, about 150g/5½oz each, skin on • 1 tbsp olive oil
Sauce 4 spring onions • 1 garlic clove • 80ml/2½fl oz fish stock • 4 tbsp vermouth
• 30g/1oz sorrel leaves • 250ml/9fl oz double cream • 1 tbsp cornflour • 1 tbsp lemon juice
• salt and freshly ground black pepper

1 To make the sauce, put the spring onions, garlic, fish stock and vermouth in the Vita-Mix machine and
   secure the 2-part lid. Select VARIABLE speed 1. Turn the machine on and increase the speed to 10, then
   to HIGH. Run for 2 minutes until the sauce is hot, then switch off the machine.
2 Add the sorrel leaves, cream, cornflour and lemon juice. Select VARIABLE speed 1. Turn the machine on
   and increase the speed to 10, then to HIGH. Run for 2 minutes until the leaves are thoroughly blended.
   Season with salt and pepper and keep warm while you cook the fish.
3 Season the fish with salt and pepper. Heat the oil in a non-stick frying pan over a medium-high heat. Put
   the fish skin-side down in the pan and press down lightly. Cook for 2 minutes until the skin is brown and
   crispy. Turn the fillets over and cook for a further 2 minutes until cooked through. Serve with the sorrel
   sauce spooned over the fish.

HEALTH BENEFITS • Energizing • Stress-busting • High protein • Low carb

Make this: *sugar-free by using fish stock instead of vermouth.*

Halibut with Romesco Sauce

SERVES 4 **PREPARATION TIME:** 10 minutes **VITA-MIX TIME:** 18 seconds
COOKING TIME: 25 minutes **SERVE WITH:** Marinated Green Beans (see page 93)
STORAGE: The sauce can be prepared in advance and kept in the fridge for 2 days. Leftovers will keep
in the fridge until the next day.

4 halibut steaks, about 125g/4½oz each • 1 tbsp olive oil
Sauce 1 red pepper, halved and deseeded • 6–7 tbsp olive oil • 1 red chilli, deseeded • 2 garlic cloves
• 1 slice of bread, about 25g/1oz, torn into chunks • 1 tomato • 50g/1¾oz toasted almonds
• 2 tbsp red wine vinegar • ½ tsp saffron strands soaked in 1 tbsp hot water

1 To make the sauce, preheat the grill to high. Put the pepper on a baking sheet and grill for 15 minutes
   or until the skin is blackened. Transfer to a bowl, cover with cling film and leave to stand until cool enough
   to handle. Once cool, remove and discard the skin.
2 Heat 2 tablespoons of the oil in a frying pan. Add the chilli, garlic and bread and fry for 2–3 minutes,
   stirring occasionally, until lightly browned. Transfer to the Vita-Mix machine, add the tomato and roasted
   pepper and secure the 2-part lid. Select VARIABLE speed 1 and run for 6–7 seconds until the mixture forms
   a smooth paste.
3 Remove the lid plug and add the almonds, vinegar and saffron. Replace the plug, select VARIABLE speed 1
   and run for 6–7 seconds until the nuts are finely ground. Scrape down the mixture from the sides of the
   container. Select VARIABLE speed 3. With the machine still running, gradually add the remaining oil and
   run for a further 3–4 seconds until smooth and thick. Transfer to a bowl.
4 To cook the fish, heat the oil in a frying pan over a medium-high heat. Add the fish and fry for
   3–4 minutes on each side until cooked through. Serve hot with the Romesco sauce spooned over the fish.

HEALTH BENEFITS • Energizing • Immune-boosting • Anti-ageing • Stress-busting • High protein
• Low carb • Low cholesterol • Low saturated fat

Tamarind Fish Curry

SERVES 4 **PREPARATION TIME:** 10 minutes, plus 30 minutes marinating
VITA-MIX TIME: 1 minute 6 seconds **COOKING TIME:** 9 minutes **SERVE WITH:** Steamed rice
STORAGE: Leftovers will keep in the fridge to the following day.

450g/1lb monkfish or swordfish fillet, cut into 1cm/½in-thick slices • 1 tbsp lemon juice • 1 onion
• 2 garlic cloves, peeled • 1cm/½in piece root ginger, peeled • 1 dried red chilli • 1½ tsp tamarind paste
• 100g/3½oz creamed coconut • 2 tomatoes • 1 tbsp olive oil • 1 tsp mustard seeds • ½ tsp turmeric
• 450g/1lb baby spinach leaves • 3 tbsp chopped coriander leaves

1 Put the fish in a shallow dish, sprinkle over the lemon juice and leave to marinate for 30 minutes.
2 Put the onion, garlic, ginger and 2 tablespoons water in the Vita-Mix machine and secure the 2-part
   lid. Select VARIABLE speed 1. Turn the machine on and increase the speed to 10. Run for 5–6 seconds
   until the mixture forms a smooth paste. Add the chilli, tamarind paste, creamed coconut, tomatoes and
   125ml/4fl oz hot water. Select VARIABLE speed 1. Turn the machine on and increase the speed to 10, then
   to HIGH. Run for 1 minute until thick.
3 Heat the oil in a saucepan over a medium heat. Add the mustard seeds and cook, stirring, for
   30 seconds until they start to pop. Add the turmeric and coconut sauce and cook for 1–2 minutes,
   stirring occasionally, until thick. Add the fish, cover and reduce the heat to low. Cook for 4–5 minutes
   until the fish is cooked through. Toss in the spinach leaves and simmer for 1–2 minutes until wilted.
   Serve sprinkled with the coriander leaves.

HEALTH BENEFITS • Energizing • Immune-boosting • High protein • Low carb

Vietnamese Tuna Salad with Lemongrass

SERVES 4 **PREPARATION TIME:** 10 minutes, plus 30 minutes chilling
VITA-MIX TIME: 1 minute 12 seconds **COOKING TIME:** 6 minutes **SERVE WITH:** A noodle salad
and Watermelon Refresher (see page 28) **STORAGE:** Prepare the dressing in advance and keep
in the fridge for up to 1 week. Leftovers will keep for up to 1 day.

600g/1lb 5oz tuna fillet, cut into 4 pieces • 1 tbsp olive oil • salt and freshly ground black pepper
Dressing 1 garlic clove • a pinch dried chilli flakes • 1 lemongrass stalk • 1cm/½in piece root ginger,
peeled • 2 tbsp Thai fish sauce • 2 tsp tamari • 3 tbsp sugar • juice of 1 lime • 2 tbsp olive oil, plus
extra as needed • freshly ground black pepper
Salad 30g/1oz salted peanuts • 1 red onion • 1 small cucumber, peeled, deseeded and sliced
• 1 carrot, peeled and cut into julienne strips • 1 red pepper, halved, deseeded and cut into julienne
strips • 3 tbsp chopped coriander leaves

1 Rub the tuna with the olive oil and season well with salt and pepper. Heat a frying pan over a high heat
   until hot, then add the fish and cook for 2–3 minutes on each side until brown on the outside but still
   slightly rare inside. Transfer to a plate and leave to cool, then cover and chill for 30 minutes.
2 Meanwhile, make the dressing. Put the garlic, chilli flakes, lemongrass and ginger in the Vita-Mix machine
   and secure the 2-part lid. Select VARIABLE speed 1 and run for 5–6 seconds until the mixture forms a
   paste. Scrape down the paste from the sides of the container into the base, add the remaining ingredients
   for the dressing and season with pepper. Secure the 2-part lid. Select VARIABLE speed 1. Turn the machine
   on and increase the speed to 10, then to HIGH. Run for 1 minute until smooth, adding a little more oil
   if the mixture is too thick. Transfer to a jug and chill until required. Wash the Vita-Mix machine.
3 Put the peanuts in the Vita-Mix machine and secure the 2-part lid. Select VARIABLE speed 1 and pulse
   on and off for 2–3 seconds until coarsely chopped. Transfer to a large bowl and set aside.
4 Put the red onion in the Vita-Mix machine and secure the 2-part lid. Select VARIABLE speed 1 and pulse
   on and off for 2–3 seconds until coarsely sliced. Add to the peanuts along with the cucumber, carrot and
   pepper. Pour over half the dressing and toss lightly, then transfer to a large serving platter.
5 Thinly slice the tuna and arrange it on top of the salad. Drizzle over a little more dressing, then scatter
   with the coriander leaves and serve.

HEALTH BENEFITS • Energizing • Immune-boosting • Anti-ageing • Stress-busting • High protein
• Low carb • Low cholesterol • Low saturated fat

Prawn Tempura with Chilli & Lime Mayonnaise

SERVES 4 **PREPARATION TIME:** 10 minutes **VITA-MIX TIME:** 34 seconds
COOKING TIME: 18 minutes **SERVE WITH:** Fennel Coleslaw in Tofu Dressing (see page 93)
STORAGE: Best eaten immediately, but the mayonnaise can be made in advance and chilled
for up to 4 days. **IF USING THE 32oz CONTAINER:** Halve the quantities.

24 raw king prawns, tails on • 25g/1oz flour • 600ml/21fl oz vegetable oil
Mayonnaise 2 eggs • ½ small red chilli, deseeded • juice of 1 lime • 150ml/5fl oz extra-virgin olive oil
• 200ml/7fl oz light vegetable oil
Batter 1 egg • 125g/4½oz plain flour • ½ tsp bicarbonate of soda

1 To make the mayonnaise, put the eggs, chilli and lime juice in the Vita-Mix machine and secure the
  2-part lid. Select VARIABLE speed 1. Turn the machine on and increase the speed to 6. While the machine
  is running, remove the lid plug, pour the oil in slowly and blend for 30 seconds until thick. Transfer to
  a bowl, cover and chill until required. Wash the Vita-Mix machine.
2 Dry the prawns well, then dust in the flour and set aside. Put the ingredients for the batter in the Vita-Mix
  machine, add 225ml/7¾fl oz ice-cold sparkling water and secure the 2-part lid. Select VARIABLE speed 1,
  turn the machine on and increase the speed to 10, then to HIGH. Run for 3–4 seconds until well mixed.
3 Heat the oil in a deep saucepan or deep fat fryer to 180°C/350°F. Working in batches, dip the prawns in
  the batter and carefully drop them into the oil. Fry for 3 minutes, turning occasionally, until golden, then
  remove using a slotted spoon and drain on kitchen paper. Serve immediately with the mayonnaise.

HEALTH BENEFITS • Energizing • High protein • Low carb

Thai-Spiced Coconut Mussels

SERVES 4 **PREPARATION TIME:** 15 minutes **VITA-MIX TIME:** 4 minutes 5 seconds
COOKING TIME: 6 minutes **SERVE WITH:** Rice noodles or steamed rice
STORAGE: The sauce can be prepared in advance and kept in the fridge for up to 2 days.
Mussels are best cooked and eaten on the day of purchase, although leftovers will keep
in the fridge until the next day.

1.5kg/3lb 5oz mussels • 30g/1oz butter • 2 shallots, finely chopped • 1 garlic clove, chopped
• 1 lemongrass stalk, finely chopped • 2 kaffir lime leaves, shredded • 1 red chilli, deseeded
and chopped • 150ml/5fl oz white wine • 2 spring onions, diagonally sliced, to serve
• 2 tbsp chopped coriander leaves, to serve • zest of 1 lime, to serve
Sauce a large pinch saffron strands • 250ml/9fl oz coconut milk • 1 tbsp cornflour
• 1 tbsp Thai fish sauce• 2 tsp demerara sugar • 1 tsp ground lemongrass • juice and zest
of 1 lime • 1 tomato, quartered • ½ red pepper, deseeded and quartered • ½ red chilli,
deseeded and shredded

1 Put the saffron for the sauce in a small bowl. Cover with 1 tablespoon boiling water and leave
   to soak for 10 minutes.
2 Meanwhile, wash the mussels, scraping the shells to remove any barnacles and pulling away any
   beards. Discard those that do not close completely when tapped.
3 Melt the butter in a large saucepan over a medium heat and add the shallots, garlic, lemongrass,
   lime leaves and chilli. Cook gently for 3 minutes, stirring occasionally, then add the mussels and wine.
   Cover with a tight-fitting lid and cook for 2 minutes until the mussels start to open, then remove
   from the heat. Discard any that have not opened.
4 To make the sauce, transfer the saffron and soaking water to the Vita-Mix machine and add the coconut
   milk, cornflour, fish sauce, sugar, ground lemongrass and lime juice and zest in the Vita-Mix machine
   in the order listed and secure the 2-part lid. Select VARIABLE speed 2. Turn the machine on and increase
   the speed to 10, then to HIGH. Run for 4 minutes or until the sauce warms through and starts to thicken.
5 Select VARIABLE speed 2 and, with the machine running, remove the lid plug and add the tomato
   and red pepper. Pulse on and off a few times until finely chopped.
6 Pour the sauce into the pan with the mussels. Add the shredded chilli and heat over a medium heat
   for 1 minute until warmed through. Sprinkle with the spring onions, coriander leaves and lime zest
   and serve immediately.

HEALTH BENEFITS • Energizing • Immune boosting • High protein • Low carb

Make this: dairy-free by using 2 tablespoons olive oil instead of butter.

Thai Green Chicken Curry

SERVES 4 **PREPARATION TIME:** 15 minutes, plus 30 minutes marinating
VITA-MIX TIME: 34 seconds **COOKING TIME:** 30 minutes
SERVE WITH: Mango chutney, flatbreads and a mixed leafy green salad
STORAGE: Make the curry paste in advance and keep in the fridge for up to 1 week. Leftovers will keep in the fridge for up to 2 days.

1 red onion • 1 garlic clove • 4 skinless, boneless chicken breasts, about 150g/5½oz each, cut into chunks • 400ml/14fl oz coconut milk • 2 tbsp olive oil• 2 dried kaffir lime leaves • 1 tbsp Thai fish sauce • 1 tbsp tamari • 2 tsp chilli sauce • 50g/1¾oz frozen peas • 150g/5½oz trimmed mangetout • 225g/8oz tinned bamboo shoots, drained and rinsed • 3 tbsp chopped coriander leaves, to serve
Curry paste 1 green chilli, deseeded • 1 shallot • 1cm/½in piece root ginger, peeled • 2 dried kaffir lime leaves • 1 lemongrass stalk • ½ tsp ground cumin • ½ tsp ground coriander • ½ tsp salt • 1 handful coriander leaves • ½ tsp shrimp paste • 4 tbsp olive oil • 1 tbsp lime juice

1 Put the red onion and garlic in the Vita-Mix machine and secure the 2-part lid. Select VARIABLE speed 1 and run for 2–3 seconds until finely chopped, then transfer to a bowl. Wash the Vita-Mix machine.
2 To make the curry paste, put all the ingredients in the Vita-Mix machine and select VARIABLE speed 1. Run for 5–6 seconds, then scrape down the mixture from the sides of the container using a spatula. Select VARIABLE speed 1. Turn the machine on and gradually increase the speed to 10, then to HIGH. Run for a further 10–15 seconds until the mixture forms a paste.
3 Put the chicken pieces in a shallow dish and spoon 1 tablespoon of the paste over them. Cover and leave to marinate for 30 minutes.
4 Add the coconut milk to the rest of the curry paste in the Vita-Mix machine and secure the 2–part lid. Select VARIABLE speed 1. Turn the machine on and increase the speed to 10, then to HIGH. Run for 10 seconds until thoroughly combined.
5 Heat the oil over a medium-high heat in a non-stick frying pan. Add the onion and garlic and cook for 2 minutes until softened. Add the chicken and fry for 5 minutes, stirring frequently, until the chicken begins to brown.
6 Add the spiced coconut milk and the kaffir lime leaves and bring to the boil. Reduce the heat to medium-low and simmer gently for 15 minutes until the chicken is tender. Stir in the fish sauce, tamari, chilli sauce, peas, mangetout and bamboo shoots. Simmer for a further 5 minutes until the vegetables are heated through but still crisp. Sprinkle with the coriander leaves and serve.

HEALTH BENEFITS • Energizing • Immune-boosting • Stress-busting • High protein

Make this: vegetarian by using tofu instead of chicken and omitting the fish sauce and shrimp paste.

Chorizo & Feta-Stuffed Chicken

SERVES 4 **PREPARATION TIME:** 20 minutes **VITA-MIX TIME:** 1 minute **COOKING TIME:** 50 minutes
SERVE WITH: A rocket salad or wilted greens **STORAGE:** Make the stuffing and fill the chicken breasts
1 day ahead. Cover and chill until ready to cook. Leftovers will keep in the fridge for up to 2 days. The
sauce can be frozen for up to 1 month.

4 chicken breasts with skin, about 150g/5½oz each • 1 tbsp olive oil • 1 lemon, thinly sliced
• 200ml/7fl oz chicken stock • 1 red pepper, quartered and deseeded • ½ red onion, sliced
Stuffing 125g/4½oz chorizo sausage, skin removed, chopped • ½ red onion • 125g/4½oz feta cheese
• 2 basil sprigs • 1 slice of bread • 2 sun-dried tomatoes in oil, drained • 1 egg, beaten • zest of 1 lemon
• salt and freshly ground black pepper

1 Preheat the oven to 200°C/400°F/Gas 6. To make the stuffing, put the chorizo and red onion in the
Vita-Mix machine. Secure the 2-part lid, select VARIABLE speed 2 and run for 20 seconds until well mixed,
using the tamper to push the ingredients into the blades. Transfer to a frying pan and cook over a low
heat, stirring occasionally, for 5 minutes. Transfer to a bowl and leave to cool. Wash the Vita-Mix machine.

2 Put the feta and basil in the Vita-Mix machine and secure the 2-part lid. Select VARIABLE speed 2 and
pulse on and off a few times until finely chopped, then add it to the chorizo.

3 Secure the 2-part lid on the Vita-Mix and select VARIABLE speed 2. Turn the machine on and, with the lid
plug removed, feed the bread and sun-dried tomatoes into the container, using the tamper to push them
into the blades. Run for 5 seconds or until fine breadcrumbs form, then add to the chorizo, along with
the egg and lemon zest. Season with salt and pepper and mix well. Wash the Vita-Mix machine.

4 Make a horizontal slit three-quarters of the way through each chicken breast to form a pocket. Divide the
stuffing into the pockets and secure with string or a cocktail stick. Put them in a roasting tin, drizzle with
the oil and top with the lemon slices. Add the chicken stock and tuck the red pepper and onion around
the chicken. Bake for 40–45 minutes until the chicken is cooked through and golden brown.

5 Transfer the chicken and lemon to a plate and leave to rest for 5 minutes. Pour the pan juices, pepper
and onion into the Vita-Mix machine and secure the 2-part lid. Select VARIABLE speed 1. Turn the machine
on and increase the speed to 10, then to HIGH. Run for 30 seconds until smooth and thick. Serve with the
chicken and lemon.

HEALTH BENEFITS • Energizing • Stress-busting • High protein • Low carb

Caribbean Baked Chicken

SERVES 4 **PREPARATION TIME:** 10 minutes, plus at least 2–3 hours marinating
VITA-MIX TIME: 16 seconds **COOKING TIME:** 35 minutes
SERVE WITH: Flatbread or steamed rice and a leafy green salad
STORAGE: Leftovers will keep in the fridge for up to 2 days.

8 chicken thighs with skin • 2 tbsp olive oil • 2 thyme sprigs • 4 tomatoes, quartered
• 1 red onion quartered
Spice paste 2 tsp allspice berries • 1 habanero or Scotch bonnet chilli • 4 spring onions
• 3 shallots • 1 garlic clove • 1cm/½in piece root ginger, peeled • a pinch cinnamon • 4 tbsp olive oil
• 1 tbsp lemon juice • 1 tsp sugar • a pinch salt • freshly ground black pepper

1 Put the ingredients for the spice paste in the Vita-Mix machine, season with pepper and secure the 2-part lid. Select VARIABLE speed 1 and run for 5–6 seconds until chopped. Scrape down the mixture from the sides of the container. Select VARIABLE speed 3. Turn the machine on and increase the speed to 10, then to HIGH. Run for 10 seconds until the mixture forms a smooth paste.
2 Rub the paste all over the chicken thighs and put them in a shallow container. Cover and chill for 2–3 hours or in the fridge overnight.
3 Preheat the oven to 180°C/350°F/Gas 4. Heat 1 tablespoon of the olive oil in a roasting tin. Add the chicken thighs and the marinade and drizzle with the remaining oil. Scatter the thyme sprigs in the tin and bake for 15 minutes, then scatter the tomatoes and onion into the tin. Roast for a further 15–20 minutes until the chicken is cooked through and golden. Serve immediately.

HEALTH BENEFITS • Energizing • Immune-boosting • Stress-busting • High protein • Low carb

Indonesian Chicken Rendang

SERVES 4 **PREPARATION TIME:** 10 minutes, plus at least 1 hour marinating
VITA-MIX TIME: 40 seconds **COOKING TIME:** 25 minutes
SERVE WITH: Steamed rice and wilted greens **STORAGE:** This can be kept in the fridge for up to 2 days.

3 tbsp olive oil • 1 tsp ground coriander • 1 tsp ground cumin • 1 tsp turmeric • ½ tsp paprika
• 1 tsp sugar • a pinch salt • 8 chicken thighs • 1 lemongrass stalk • 3 shallots • 1 garlic clove
• 1cm/½in piece root ginger, peeled • 60g/2¼oz desiccated coconut • 300ml/10½oz coconut milk
• 2 tsp lime juice • 3 tbsp chopped coriander leaves • zest of 1 lime

1 In a small bowl, mix together 1 tablespoon of the olive oil, the ground coriander, cumin, turmeric, paprika, sugar and salt and rub this mixture over the chicken thighs. Put them in a shallow bowl, cover and leave to marinate for at least 1 hour.
2 Put the lemongrass, shallots, garlic, ginger and 1 tablespoon water in the Vita-Mix machine and secure the 2-part lid. Select VARIABLE speed 1. Turn the machine on and increase the speed to 3. Run for 4–5 seconds. Scrape down the mixture into the blades and run for a further 4–5 seconds until the mixture forms a coarse paste.
3 Put the coconut in a non-stick frying pan over a medium-high heat and cook for 3–4 minutes, stirring, until golden. Add the coconut and coconut milk to the spice paste in the Vita-Mix machine. Select VARIABLE Speed 1. Turn the machine on and increase the speed to 10, then to HIGH. Run for 20–30 seconds until smooth.
4 Heat the remaining oil in a large non-stick frying pan over a medium-high heat. Add the chicken and fry for 2 minutes on each side until lightly golden. Add the coconut sauce and simmer, covered, over a low heat for 20 minutes until the chicken is cooked through. Stir in the lime juice and coriander leaves and serve sprinkled with the lime zest.

HEALTH BENEFITS • Energizing • Immune-boosting • Stress-busting • High protein • Low carb

Make this: vegetarian by using cubes of firm tofu instead of the chicken. Make this sugar-free by omitting the sugar and using unsweetened desiccated coconut.

Spicy Sesame Chicken Noodles

SERVES 4 **PREPARATION TIME:** 15 minutes, plus at least 1 hour marinating
VITA-MIX TIME: 13 seconds **COOKING TIME:** 15 minutes **SERVE WITH:** Wilted greens
or stir-fried pak choi **STORAGE:** This can be kept in the fridge for up to 2 days.

1 tbsp sesame seeds • 350g/12oz chicken breast fillets, sliced into thin strips • 200g/7oz noodles
• 2 shallots • ½ small red chilli, deseeded • 1 garlic clove • 1 tsp pickled ginger • 3 tbsp lemon juice
• 2 tbsp tamari • 2 tsp caster sugar • 2 tbsp olive oil • 100g/3½oz bean sprouts • 4 shiitake mushrooms,
sliced • 100g/3½oz mangetout, trimmed • 1 red pepper, halved, deseeded and cut into strips
• 2 tbsp chopped coriander leaves
Marinade 1 shallot • 3 tbsp sake or sherry • 90ml/3fl oz tamari • 3 tbsp mirin • 1 tsp caster sugar

1 Heat a non-stick frying pan over a medium-high heat and add the sesame seeds. Cook for 1 minute,
stirring continuously, until golden brown. Transfer to a bowl and set aside.
2 Put the ingredients for the marinade in the Vita-Mix machine and secure the 2-part lid. Select VARIABLE
speed 1 and run for 5–6 seconds until blended. Put the chicken in a bowl and pour the marinade over.
Toss to coat and leave to marinate for at least 1 hour. Wash the Vita-Mix machine.
3 Bring a large pan of water to the boil and cook the noodles for 2–3 minutes or until just tender. Drain,
then rinse under cold running water and set aside.
4 Put the shallots, chilli, garlic, ginger, lemon juice, tamari and sugar in the Vita-Mix machine and secure the
2-part lid. Select VARIABLE speed 1 and run for 6–7 seconds until the mixture forms a coarse paste. Scrape
down the mixture into the blades if necessary to blend thoroughly.
5 Heat a large wok or non-stick frying pan over a medium heat and add the oil. Add the chicken,
marinade and spice paste and stir-fry for 4 minutes until lightly brown. Add the bean sprouts, mushrooms,
mangetout and pepper and stir-fry for a further 2–3 minutes. Toss in the noodles and cook for a further
2 minutes, stirring occasionally, until everything is just tender and heated through. Sprinkle with the
sesame seeds and coriander leaves and serve immediately.

HEALTH BENEFITS • Energizing • Immune-boosting • Stress-busting • High protein

Make this: *gluten-free by using rice or buckwheat noodles. Make this vegetarian by using cubes
of firm tofu instead of chicken.*

Stir-Fried Turkey with Pak Choi

SERVES 4 **PREPARATION TIME:** 10 minutes **VITA-MIX TIME:** 12 seconds
COOKING TIME: 11 minutes **SERVE WITH:** Steamed broccoli **STORAGE:** Leftovers will keep
in the fridge for up to 2 days.

1 red onion • ½ red chilli, deseeded • 2 tbsp tamari • 2cm/¾in piece root ginger, peeled • 1 garlic
clove • juice and zest of 1 lime • 1 tbsp Thai fish sauce • 250g/9oz rice noodles • 2 tbsp olive oil
• 450g/1lb turkey breast fillets, cut into strips • 200g/7oz pak choi, roughly chopped • 1 red pepper,
halved, deseeded and cut into strips • 1 carrot, peeled and cut into strips • 6 baby sweetcorn, cut
in half lengthways • 60g/2¼oz bean sprouts

1 Put the onion and chilli in the Vita-Mix machine and secure the 2-part lid. Select VARIABLE speed 1 and
run for 6–7 seconds until finely chopped. Transfer to a bowl and set aside. Wash the Vita-Mix machine.
2 Put the tamari, ginger, garlic, lime juice and zest and fish sauce in the Vita-Mix machine and secure the
2-part lid. Select VARIABLE speed 1. Turn the machine on and increase the speed to 10, then to HIGH.
Run for 5 seconds until smooth, then set aside.
3 Bring a pan of water to the boil and cook the rice noodles according to the packet instructions. Drain
under cold running water and set aside.
4 Meanwhile, heat the oil in a large wok or non-stick frying pan over a medium-high heat. Add the onion
and chilli and stir-fry for 1 minute, then add the turkey and cook for 3–4 minutes, stirring frequently, until
brown. Add the vegetables and stir-fry for 3–4 minutes until the vegetables begin to soften.
5 Toss in the noodles and sauce and cook for a further 2 minutes until heated through. Serve immediately.

HEALTH BENEFITS • Energizing • Immune-boosting • Stress-busting • High Protein • Low cholesterol
• Low saturated fat • Low calorie • Low kilojoule

Turkey, Mushroom
& Pancetta Potato Pie

SERVES 4 **PREPARATION TIME:** 15 minutes **VITA-MIX TIME:** 5 minutes 15 seconds
COOKING TIME: 55 minutes **SERVE WITH:** Steamed leafy greens or mixed salad
STORAGE: The pie can be prepared in advance and kept unbaked in the fridge for up to 1 day.
Leftovers will keep in the fridge for up to 2 days.

600g/1lb 5oz turkey breast fillets, diced • 1 leek, sliced • 600ml/21fl oz chicken stock • 1 onion
• 1 garlic clove • 2 tbsp olive oil • 110g/3¾oz chestnut mushrooms, sliced • 110g/3¾oz pancetta, diced
Sauce 200ml/7fl oz full-fat milk • 40g/1½oz butter • 40g/1½oz plain flour • 3–4 flat-leaf parsley sprigs
• freshly ground black pepper
Mash 1kg/2lb 4oz floury potatoes, peeled and cut into chunks • 200ml/7fl oz full-fat milk
• 1 tbsp olive oil

1 Preheat the oven to 200°C/400°F/Gas 6. Put the turkey, leek and chicken stock in a pan. Bring to the boil
   over a high heat, then reduce the heat to low and simmer, covered, for 15 minutes.
2 Meanwhile, to make the mash, bring a large pan of salted water to the boil and add the potatoes. Simmer
   for 15 minutes until tender, then drain. Put the milk in a pan and heat over a medium heat for 2 minutes,
   stirring occasionally, until hot. Transfer the milk to the Vita-Mix machine and add the oil and potatoes.
   Secure the 2-part lid and select VARIABLE speed 1. Turn the machine on and increase the speed to 6.
   Use the tamper to push the potatoes into the blades. Run for 6–7 seconds until smooth. Transfer the mash
   to a bowl and set aside. Wash the Vita-Mix machine.
3 Drain the turkey and leek through a colander and reserve the stock. Transfer the turkey and leek
   to a large bowl.
4 Put the onion and garlic in the Vita-Mix machine and secure the 2-part lid. Select VARIABLE speed 1 and
   run for 3–4 seconds until coarsely chopped. Transfer to a bowl and set aside. Wash the Vita-Mix machine.
5 Heat the oil in a large non-stick frying pan over a medium-high heat. Add the onion and garlic and cook
   for 1 minute, stirring, until beginning to soften. Add the mushrooms and pancetta and cook for a further
   2 minutes, stirring occasionally, until the pancetta begins to turn lightly golden. Remove from the heat
   and add to the turkey. Mix well.
6 To make the sauce, put the milk in a pan and heat over a medium heat for 2 minutes, stirring occasionally,
   until hot. Transfer the milk to the Vita-Mix machine and add the butter, flour and 100ml/3½fl oz of the
   reserved turkey stock. Season with pepper and secure the 2-part lid. Select VARIABLE speed 1. Turn the
   machine on and increase the speed to 10, then to HIGH. Run for 5 minutes until hot and steaming, then
   add the parsley. Select VARIABLE speed 1 and pulse on and off to chop the parsley. Pour the sauce over
   the turkey mixture and mix well.
7 Spoon the turkey mixture into a large pie dish. Spread the mashed potato over the top and bake for
   30–35 minutes until the potato is lightly golden. Serve immediately.

HEALTH BENEFITS • Energizing • Stress-busting • High protein

Griddled Duck with Sour Cherry & Red Wine Sauce

SERVES 4 **PREPARATION TIME:** 10 minutes, plus at least 1 hour marinating
VITA-MIX TIME: 5 minutes 5 seconds **COOKING TIME:** 14 minutes **SERVE WITH:** Herb Mash
(see page 91) and steamed greens **STORAGE:** Leftovers will keep in the fridge for up to 2 days.

4 duck breasts, about 225g/8oz each, skin on • 50g/1¾oz dried sour cherries • 3 tbsp red wine
• 2 tbsp olive oil
Marinade 2 shallots • 1 tsp sesame oil • 1 tbsp olive oil • 1 tbsp Chinese five-spice powder
• a pinch chilli powder • 1 tbsp soy sauce
Sauce 2 shallots • 100g/3½oz Morello cherry jam • 90ml/3fl oz red wine • 2 tsp cornflour

1 Put the ingredients for the marinade in the Vita-Mix machine and secure the 2-part lid. Select VARIABLE
   speed 1 and run for 4–5 seconds until combined. Using a sharp knife, make 2–3 slashes through the skin
   of each duck breast and put in a shallow dish. Pour the marinade over, then cover and chill for 1 hour
   or overnight in the fridge. Wash the Vita-Mix machine.
2 Meanwhile, put the dried cherries in a small bowl, cover with the wine and leave to soak for 30 minutes.
3 Preheat the oven to 200°C/400°F/Gas 6. Heat a griddle or frying pan over a high heat, then add the oil.
   Put the duck skin-side down in the pan and cook for 2 minutes on each side until golden brown. Transfer
   to a baking sheet and bake for 10 minutes. Remove from the oven and leave to stand for 10 minutes.
4 Put the ingredients for the sauce in the Vita-Mix machine and secure the 2-part lid. Select VARIABLE speed
   1. Turn the machine on and increase the speed to 10, then to HIGH. Run for 4–5 minutes until thick and
   steaming. Stir in the dried cherries and wine. Slice the duck breasts diagonally and serve with the sauce.

HEALTH BENEFITS • Energizing • Stress-busting • High protein

Pan-Fried Duck with Sweet Tamarind Sauce

SERVES 4 **PREPARATION TIME:** 20 minutes, plus 1 hour marinating
VITA-MIX TIME: 1 minute 7 seconds **COOKING TIME:** 20 minutes
SERVE WITH: Steamed rice and stir-fried pak choi
STORAGE: The sauce can be prepared in advance and kept in the fridge for up to 2 days. Leftovers can be kept in the fridge for up to 2 days.

2 tsp Chinese five-spice powder • 2 tbsp olive oil • 4 duck breasts, about 225g/8oz each, skin on
• salt and freshly ground black pepper
Sauce 1 tsp aniseed • 1 tsp coriander seeds • 2 shallots • 1 garlic clove • 4 tbsp peanuts
• 5 tbsp soft brown sugar or palm sugar • a pinch salt • a pinch chilli powder • 1 tbsp tamarind paste
• 2 tbsp Thai fish sauce • 3 tbsp sultanas • 3 sprigs coriander leaves

1 In a small bowl, mix together the five-spice powder and 1 tablespoon of the olive oil and rub this over the duck breasts. Put them in a shallow bowl, cover and marinate in the fridge for 1 hour.
2 Meanwhile, heat a small frying pan over a medium-high heat. Add the aniseed and coriander seeds and cook for 2–3 minutes, stirring, until toasted. Transfer to a bowl and leave to cool.
3 Preheat the oven to 200°C/400°F/Gas 6. To make the sauce, put the shallots, garlic and 1 tablespoon water in the Vita-Mix machine and secure the 2-part lid. Select VARIABLE speed 2 and run for 2–3 seconds until finely chopped. Remove the lid plug and add the peanuts, sugar, salt, chilli powder, and aniseed and coriander seeds. Continue to run for 3–4 seconds until the mixture forms a coarse paste, then scrape the mixture into the centre of the container, using a spatula.
4 Add the tamarind paste, fish sauce and 5 tablespoons water. Replace the lid plug and select VARIABLE speed 2. Turn the machine on and increase the speed to 10, then to HIGH. Run for 1 minute until the sauce is thick and creamy. Transfer to a saucepan.
5 Season the duck with salt and pepper. Heat the oil in a frying pan over a medium heat, then add the duck breasts and cook for 2 minutes on each side until brown. Transfer to a baking sheet and bake for 10–12 minutes. Remove from the oven and leave to stand for 10 minutes.
6 Gently heat the tamarind sauce over a low heat until simmering. Stir in the sultanas.
7 Slice the duck, then spoon the tamarind sauce over, sprinkle with the coriander leaves and serve.

HEALTH BENEFITS • Energizing • Stress-busting • High protein • Low carb

Make this: vegetarian by omitting the fish sauce and using tinned chickpeas instead of duck. Prepare the sauce to the end of step 4, add the chickpeas and heat over a medium heat until hot, then continue as directed. Serve with poppadoms and raita.

Moroccan Roasted Guinea Fowl Stuffed with Fruit & Nut Pilaff

SERVES 4 **PREPARATION TIME:** 10 minutes
VITA-MIX TIME: 7 seconds **COOKING TIME:** 1 hour 30 minutes
SERVE WITH: A leafy green salad and Marinated Green Beans (See page 93)
STORAGE: Prepare the stuffing in advance and chill for up to 2 days. Leftovers will keep in the fridge for up to 2 days.

2 guinea fowl, about 900g/2lb each • 3 tbsp olive oil • 1 large onion, quartered
• 1 tsp ground ginger • 1 cinnamon stick • ½ tsp turmeric • a pinch saffron strands
• 150ml/5fl oz chicken stock • 150ml/5fl oz white wine • 225g/8oz cherry tomatoes
• 2 tbsp chopped flat-leaf parsley • 1 tbsp lemon juice • salt and freshly ground
black pepper
Stuffing 100g/3½oz ready-to-eat dried dates • 1 garlic clove • 50g/1¾oz toasted almonds
• 1 preserved lemon, skin only, flesh discarded • 2 tbsp olive oil • 50g/1¾oz couscous

1 Heat the oven to 180°C/350°F/Gas 4. To make the stuffing, put the dates, garlic, almonds, preserved lemon and olive oil in the Vita-Mix machine and secure the 2-part lid. Select VARIABLE speed 3 and run for 6–7 seconds until the mixture forms a stiff paste.
2 Make the couscous according to the packet instructions, then stir it into the fruit and nut paste and season with salt and pepper.
3 Spoon the stuffing into the cavity of each guinea fowl and secure with a skewer or cocktail stick. Put the guinea fowl in a large roasting tin and drizzle over the oil. Put the onion and spices in the roasting tin and pour over the chicken stock.
4 Bake for 45 minutes, spooning over the released juices occasionally to baste. Add the wine and tomatoes and continue to bake for a further 30–35 minutes until the guinea fowl is crispy and cooked through.
5 Transfer the guinea fowl and tomatoes to a serving platter and leave to rest for 15 minutes.
6 Put the roasting tin on the hob over a medium heat and simmer for 5 minutes. Strain into a clean pan, then add the parsley and lemon juice and season with salt and pepper.
7 Slice the guinea fowl and serve with the tomatoes and sauce.

HEALTH BENEFITS • Energizing • Stress-busting • High protein

Make this: *gluten- and wheat-free by using quinoa instead of couscous.*

Spicy Roast Lamb
with Mango Sauce

SERVES 4–6 **PREPARATION TIME:** 20 minutes, plus at least 1 hour marinating
VITA-MIX TIME: 12 seconds **COOKING TIME:** 1 hour 35 minutes
SERVE WITH: Brown basmati rice and wilted leafy greens
STORAGE: Leftovers will keep in the fridge for up to 3 days.

1 small leg of lamb, about 1kg/2lb 4oz • 1cm/½in piece root ginger, peeled • 2 garlic cloves
• ½ tsp turmeric • a pinch dried chilli flakes • 5 tbsp olive oil • 3 onions • 1 tsp mustard seeds
• 1 tsp cumin seeds • 5 cloves • 1 tsp garam masala • 1 tsp ground coriander • a pinch salt
• a pinch sugar • 1 tbsp tomato purée • 1 mango, peeled, pitted and cut into cubes
• 150ml/5fl oz lamb stock • 3 tbsp chopped coriander leaves

1 Using a sharp knife, make a few deep cuts in the surface of the lamb. Put the ginger, garlic, turmeric, chilli flakes and 4 tablespoons of the olive oil in the Vita-Mix machine and secure the 2-part lid. Select VARIABLE speed 1 and run for 5 seconds until the mixture forms a paste. Rub the paste all over the lamb, put it in a shallow dish, cover and leave to marinate in the fridge for 1 hour or overnight.
2 Preheat the oven to 180°C/350°F/Gas 4. Put the onions and 1 tablespoon water in the Vita-Mix machine and secure the 2-part lid. Select VARIABLE speed 1 and run for 6–7 seconds until the mixture forms a paste.
3 Heat the remaining oil over a medium heat in a roasting tin or casserole dish large enough to hold the lamb. Add the mustard and cumin seeds and cook for 20 seconds until they start to sizzle. Stir in the onions, cloves, garam masala, ground coriander, salt, sugar and tomato purée. Add the lamb and cook for 1 minute on each side until brown. Scatter the mango into the dish, pour the stock over and cover the pan with foil.
4 Bake for 1½ hours until the lamb is tender and cooked through, turning the lamb over halfway through the cooking. Add a little water during baking if it becomes too dry.
5 Transfer the lamb to a large plate and leave to rest for 15 minutes. Put the casserole dish on the hob and simmer over a medium-low heat for 2 minutes until the juices thicken slightly. Stir in the coriander leaves. Slice the lamb and spoon the sauce over to serve.

HEALTH BENEFITS • Energizing • Immune-boosting • Stress-busting • High protein • Low carb

Make this: sugar-free by omitting the sugar.

Lamb Tagine with Chermoula Paste

SERVES 4 **PREPARATION TIME:** 20 minutes **VITA-MIX TIME:** 27 seconds
COOKING TIME: 1 hour 15 minutes **SERVE WITH:** Millet or quinoa
STORAGE: Leftovers will keep in the fridge for up to 2 days.

Paste 1 garlic clove • 1 handful flat-leaf parsley • 1 handful coriander leaves • ½ tsp paprika
• ½ tsp ground cumin • a pinch dried chilli flakes • 1 tsp ground coriander • ½ tsp cinnamon
• 4 tbsp olive oil • 2 tsp lemon juice • 350g/12oz tomatoes
Tagine 1 onion • 2 tbsp olive oil • 500g/1lb 2oz boneless lean lamb, diced • 350ml/12fl oz lamb stock
• a pinch saffron strands • 3 tbsp ground almonds • 1 sweet potato, peeled and cut into chunks
• 1 red pepper, halved, deseeded and cut into chunks • 1 yellow pepper, halved, deseeded and cut into
chunks • 60g/2¼oz ready-to-eat dried apricots • 60g/2¼oz ready-to-eat dried dates • 3 tbsp flat-leaf
parsley leaves, chopped • 3 tbsp toasted flaked almonds • salt and freshly ground black pepper

1 Put all the ingredients for the paste, except the tomatoes, in the Vita-Mix machine. Secure the
   2-part lid. Select VARIABLE speed 1 and run for 6–7 seconds. Scrape down the mixture from the sides
   of the container using a spatula and run for a further 6–7 seconds until the mixture forms a paste.
   Add the tomatoes and secure the 2-part lid. Select VARIABLE speed 1. Turn the machine on and increase
   the speed to 10, then to HIGH. Run for 10 seconds until thick and smooth. Transfer to a bowl and set
   aside. Wash the Vita-Mix machine.
2 To make the tagine, put the onion in the Vita-Mix machine and secure the 2-part lid. Select VARIABLE
   speed 1 and pulse on and off 2–3 times until finely chopped.
3 Heat the oil in a large ovenproof casserole dish over a medium heat. Add the onion and lamb and
   lightly fry for 5–6 minutes, stirring occasionally, until brown all over. Add the tomato mixture, lamb stock,
   saffron and ground almonds. Bring to a simmer, cover and cook for 40 minutes until thickened.
4 Preheat the oven to 180°C/350°F/Gas 4. Add the sweet potato, peppers, apricots and dates and
   season with salt and pepper. Bake for 30 minutes until the lamb is cooked through. Check occasionally
   during cooking, adding a little water if it becomes too dry. Scatter over the parsley and toasted
   almonds and serve.

HEALTH BENEFITS • Energizing • Immune-boosting • Stress-busting • High protein • Low carb

Make this: vegetarian and vegan by using 400g/14oz tinned chickpeas instead of lamb and vegetable
stock instead of lamb stock.

Crispy Lamb-Filled Filo Parcels

SERVES 4–6 **PREPARATION TIME:** 20 minutes
VITA-MIX TIME: 21 seconds **COOKING TIME:** 30 minutes
SERVE WITH: Tomato relish or cucumber and mint raita and a leafy green salad
STORAGE: These will keep in the fridge until the following day.

1 shallot • 1 tbsp olive oil • 400g/14oz lean lamb fillet, cut into chunks • a pinch paprika • a pinch cayenne pepper • 200g/7oz feta cheese • 2 sprigs mint • 16 filo pastry sheets, about 16 x 13cm/6¼ x 5in • 25g/1oz butter, melted • freshly ground black pepper

1 Preheat the oven to 220°C/425°F/Gas 7. Put the shallot in the Vita-Mix machine and secure the 2-part lid. Select VARIABLE speed 3 and run for 4–5 seconds until finely chopped.
2 Heat the oil in a large non-stick frying pan over a medium heat. Add the lamb and shallot and fry for 2–3 minutes, stirring occasionally, until lightly browned. Add the paprika and cayenne pepper and cook for a further 8 minutes until the lamb is cooked through. Remove from the heat and leave to cool slightly. Wash the Vita-Mix machine.
3 Put the lamb and shallot in the Vita-Mix machine and secure the 2-part lid. Select VARIABLE speed 1 and run for 7–8 seconds until the meat is finely chopped. Use the tamper to push the meat into the blades. Transfer the mixture to a bowl and wash the Vita-Mix machine.
4 Put the feta and mint in the Vita-Mix machine and secure the 2-part lid. Select VARIABLE speed 1. Turn the machine on and run for 7–8 seconds until finely chopped. Add the cheese and mint to the lamb and mix well, then season with a little pepper.
5 Put a sheet of filo pastry on a work surface and brush with a little melted butter. Place a little of the mixture along the long side of the filo, leaving a margin on either side. Roll up into a log, tucking in the sides as you roll. Repeat with the rest of the filo and filling to make 16 parcels.
6 Brush the tops of the filo parcels with melted butter and put them on a baking sheet. Bake for 15 minutes until golden. Serve warm.

HEALTH BENEFITS • Energizing • Stress-busting • High protein • Low carb

Make this: vegetarian by omitting the lamb and feta cheese and using 300g/10½oz wilted baby spinach mixed with 250g/9oz ricotta cheese and a sprinkling of Parmesan cheese and grated lemon zest. Make this dairy-free by using soya cheese and olive oil instead of feta cheese and butter. Make this lower in saturated fat by using a reduced-fat feta cheese and using olive oil instead of butter to brush the filo parcels.

Ricotta, Broccoli & Parma Ham Calzone

SERVES 4 **PREPARATION TIME:** 20 minutes, plus 1 hour rising **VITA-MIX TIME:** 5 seconds
COOKING TIME: 18 minutes **SERVE WITH:** A leafy green salad
STORAGE: These will keep in the fridge for up to 3 days.

Dough 225g/8oz strong white bread flour, plus extra for kneading the dough • a pinch salt
• 125ml/4fl oz milk • 1 tsp fast-acting dried yeast • 1 tbsp olive oil
Filling 75g/2½oz broccoli florets • 250g/9oz ricotta cheese • 1 handful basil leaves
• 100g/3½oz Parma ham, chopped • olive oil, for brushing • freshly ground black pepper

1 To make the dough, sift the flour and salt into a bowl. Put the milk in a pan and heat over a medium heat
   for 1 minute until warm. Add the milk, yeast and oil to the flour and mix to form a soft dough. Turn onto
   a lightly floured surface and knead for 10 minutes until smooth and elastic. Transfer to a clean bowl, cover
   with cling film and leave to rise in a warm place for 1 hour until doubled in size.
2 Preheat the oven to 200°C/400°F/Gas 6 and put a baking sheet in the oven. Put the broccoli in a steamer
   and steam for 3 minutes – it should still be crisp. Put the ricotta, basil and broccoli in the Vita-Mix machine
   and secure the 2-part lid. Select VARIABLE speed 1 and pulse on and off 2–3 times until coarsely chopped.
   Transfer to a bowl, add the Parma ham and mix well, then season with pepper.
3 Knock back the dough and divide it into 4 pieces. On a lightly floured surface, roll each piece into a thin
   circle. Put one quarter of the mixture on half of each circle, leaving a margin around the edge. Brush the
   edges with a little water, then fold over and pinch together to seal. Transfer to the baking sheet and brush
   with olive oil. Bake for 10–15 minutes until crisp and golden. Serve warm.

HEALTH BENEFIT • Energizing

Pork Escalopes in Leek & Walnut Sauce

SERVES 4 **PREPARATION TIME:** 15 minutes **VITA-MIX TIME:** 23 seconds
COOKING TIME: 11 minutes **SERVE WITH:** Herb Mash (see page 91) **STORAGE:** Make the cream sauce in advance and keep chilled for up to 2 days. Leftovers will keep until the following day.
IF USING THE 32oz CONTAINER: Halve the quantities.

25g/1oz wholemeal or rye bread, about 1 small slice • 250ml/9fl oz full-fat milk • 1 leek
• 100g/3½oz walnuts • 1 garlic clove • 2 flat-leaf parsley sprigs, plus 2 tbsp chopped for sprinkling
• 6 tbsp olive oil • 3 tbsp Parmesan cheese • 4 pork escalopes, about 100g/3½oz each • 2 tbsp lemon juice • 3–4 tbsp white wine (optional) • salt and freshly ground black pepper

1 Put the bread in a shallow bowl and spoon over 4 tablespoons of the milk. Leave to soak for 5 minutes.
2 Put the leek in the Vita-Mix machine and secure the 2-part lid. Select VARIABLE speed 1. Turn the machine on and increase the speed to 3. Run for 10 seconds until finely chopped, using the tamper to press the leeks into the blades. Transfer to a bowl and set aside. Wash the Vita-Mix machine.
3 Put the soaked bread, walnuts, garlic and parsley in the Vita-Mix machine and secure the 2-part lid. Select VARIABLE speed 1. Turn the machine on and increase the speed to 10. Run for 7–8 seconds until smooth. Switch off the machine and add the rest of the milk and 5 tablespoons of the oil. Select VARIABLE speed 1. Turn the machine on and increase the speed to 10, then to HIGH. Run for 5 seconds until combined. Turn the machine off and stir in the Parmesan.
4 Wrap each of the escalopes in cling film and pound flat, then season with salt and pepper. Heat the remaining oil in a large non-stick frying pan over a medium-high heat and add the escalopes. Cook for 3 minutes on each side until brown, then add the lemon juice and leeks and cook for 2–3 minutes until softened. Add the walnut cream sauce and simmer for 2 minutes until heated through, adding a little of the wine if the mixture thickens. Serve sprinkled with the chopped parsley, if using.

HEALTH BENEFITS • Energizing • Stress-busting • High protein • Low carb • High fibre

Spanish-Style Pork Fillets with Sherry–Clementine Sauce

SERVES 4 **PREPARATION TIME:** 15 minutes **VITA-MIX TIME:** 2 minutes 14 seconds
COOKING TIME: 35 minutes **SERVE WITH:** Herb Mash (see page 91) and steamed vegetables
STORAGE: Leftovers will keep in the fridge for up to 2 days.
IF USING THE 32oz CONTAINER: Halve the quantities.

2 onions • 4 clementines, peeled • 2 shallots • 1 garlic clove • 230ml/7¾fl oz sherry • 1 tbsp sherry vinegar • 1 tbsp cornflour • 4 pork fillets, about 125g/4½oz each • 1 tbsp flour • 2 tbsp olive oil
• 1 red pepper, halved, deseeded and chopped • 150g/5½oz button mushrooms • 60g/2¼oz pitted black olives • 3 tbsp chopped flat-leaf parsley • salt and freshly ground black pepper

1 Put the onions in the Vita-Mix machine, cover with water and secure the 2-part lid. Select VARIABLE speed 1 and pulse on and off a few times to chop. Drain the onions and set aside.
2 Put the clementines in the Vita-Mix machine and secure the 2-part lid. Select VARIABLE speed 3. Turn the machine on and increase the speed to 10, then to HIGH. Run for 10 seconds or until smooth. Remove the lid plug and add the shallots, garlic, sherry, vinegar and cornflour. Replace the lid plug and run on HIGH for 2 minutes until the mixture forms a warm sauce.
3 Season the pork fillets with a little salt and pepper and dust with the flour, shaking off any excess. Heat the oil in a large saucepan over a high heat. Add the pork and fry for 2 minutes on each side until lightly browned. Transfer the meat to a plate and set aside. Add the onions to the pan and cook for 2 minutes, stirring, until softened. Add the pepper and the clementine sauce and bring to a simmer.
4 Return the pork to the pan, cover and cook over a very low heat for 15 minutes. Remove the lid and add the mushrooms and olives. Cook for a further 15 minutes until the pork is cooked through and the sauce has thickened. Sprinkle over the parsley and serve.

HEALTH BENEFITS • Energizing • Immune-boosting • Stress-busting • High protein • Low carb

Chinese Chilli Beef Pancakes

SERVES 4 **PREPARATION TIME:** 20 minutes **VITA-MIX TIME:** 30 seconds
COOKING TIME: 25 minutes **SERVE WITH:** Fennel Coleslaw in Tofu Dressing (see page 93)
and thinly sliced cucumber strips. **STORAGE:** The pancakes can be made the day before and
kept in the fridge. To reheat, sprinkle with a little water and put in a hot non-stick frying pan
over a medium heat to warm through. Leftovers will keep in the fridge for 1 day.

Pancakes 250g/9oz plain flour, plus extra for rolling the dough • 2 tbsp sesame oil
Filling 1 garlic clove • a pinch dried chilli flakes • 1cm/½in piece root ginger, peeled
• 2 tbsp tamari • 3 tbsp mirin • 1 tbsp honey • 1 tbsp olive oil • 150g/5½oz lean beef fillet,
cut into thin strips • ½ red pepper, deseeded and sliced • ½ yellow pepper, deseeded
and sliced • 6 shiitake mushrooms, stems discarded, chopped • 4 spring onions, chopped
• 25g/1oz bean sprouts • coriander leaves, to serve

1 To make the pancakes, put the flour, 1 tablespoon of the sesame oil and 185ml/6fl oz boiling
   water in the Vita-Mix machine and secure the 2-part lid. Select VARIABLE speed 1. Turn the machine
   on and increase the speed to 10, then to HIGH and pulse on and off 10–15 times until the mixture
   forms a soft dough. Remove from the Vita-Mix and roll into a long log. Cut into 8 pieces of equal
   size and, on a lightly floured surface, roll out into thin pancakes. Brush each side with the remaining
   sesame oil. Wash the Vita-Mix machine.
2 Put the garlic, chilli flakes, ginger, tamari, mirin and honey in the Vita-Mix machine and secure the
   2-part lid. Select VARIABLE speed 1. Turn the machine on and increase the speed to 10, then to HIGH.
   Run for 20 seconds or until the mixture forms a sauce.
3 Heat the oil in a frying pan or wok over a medium heat. Add the beef and stir-fry for 2–3 minutes.
   Add the peppers, mushrooms and spring onions and continue to stir-fry for 2 minutes, then add
   the sauce and bean sprouts and cook for a further 2 minutes, stirring. Keep warm while you cook
   the pancakes.
4 Heat a non-stick frying pan over a medium heat until hot. Cook the pancakes for 1 minute on each
   side until very lightly coloured, then transfer to a wire rack while you cook the remaining pancakes.
5 Divide the beef filling evenly onto one half of each pancake and fold the pancakes over the filling.
   Sprinkle with coriander leaves and serve.

HEALTH BENEFITS • Energizing • Immune-boosting • Stress-busting • High protein

Make this: vegetarian by using tofu instead of beef. Make this wheat- and gluten-free by using
a wheat- and gluten-free flour instead of plain flour to make the pancakes. Make this seed-free
by using olive oil instead of sesame oil.

Desserts

Vanilla Ice Cream

Vanilla Ice Cream

SERVES 4 **PREPARATION TIME:** 5 minutes **VITA-MIX TIME:** 30 seconds
FREEZING TIME: 6 hours **SERVE WITH:** Raspberry & Plum Crumble (see page 149) or apple pie
STORAGE: Put in a shallow freezerproof container and freeze for up to 3 months. Remove from the freezer 30 minutes before serving to allow it to soften slightly.
IF USING THE 32oz CONTAINER: Halve the quantities.

500ml/17fl oz vanilla-flavoured milk • 100ml/3½fl oz double cream • 55ml/1¾fl oz single cream
• 1 tbsp sugar • 1 tbsp vanilla extract

1 Pour the vanilla-flavoured milk into a shallow freezerproof container and freeze for 6 hours or until frozen. After 2–3 hours into the freezing time, use a knife to cut the milk into ice-cube-sized pieces, then continue to freeze.
2 Put the double cream, single cream, sugar, vanilla extract and frozen milk cubes in the Vita-Mix machine in that order and secure the 2-part lid. Select VARIABLE speed 1. Turn the machine on and increase the speed to 10, then to HIGH, using the tamper to push the ingredients into the blades.
3 In about 30 seconds the sound of the motor will change and 4 mounds should form in the mixture. Stop the machine and serve immediately.

HEALTH BENEFITS • Energizing • High protein • Low carb

Cinnamon, Banana & Almond Ice Cream

SERVES 4 **PREPARATION TIME:** 5 minutes, plus 4–5 hours for freezing the bananas
VITA-MIX TIME: 1 minute **STORAGE:** Put in a shallow freezerproof container and freeze for up to 3 months. Remove from the freezer 40 minutes before serving to allow it to soften slightly.
IF USING THE 32oz CONTAINER: Halve the quantities.

100g/3½oz blanched almonds • 2 tbsp sugar • 2 tsp cinnamon • 2 tsp vanilla extract
• 4 bananas, frozen • 24 ice cubes

1 Put the almonds and 200ml/7fl oz water in the Vita-Mix machine and secure the 2-part lid. Select VARIABLE speed 1. Turn the machine on and increase the speed to 10, then to HIGH. Run for 30 seconds or until smooth.
2 With the machine still running, remove the lid plug and add the remaining ingredients in the order listed, using the tamper to push them into the blades.
3 In about 30 seconds, the sound of the motor will change and 4 mounds should form in the mixture. Stop the machine and serve immediately.

HEALTH BENEFITS • Energizing • Anti-ageing • Weight-shifting • High fibre • Low cholesterol
• Low saturated fat

Chocolate & Cherry Tofu Ice Cream

SERVES 4 **PREPARATION TIME:** 15 minutes **VITA-MIX TIME:** 1 minute **FREEZING TIME:** 4–5 hours
STORAGE: Put in a shallow freezerproof container and freeze for up to 3 months. Remove from the
freezer 40 minutes before serving to allow it to soften slightly.
IF USING THE 32oz CONTAINER: Halve the quantities.

300g/10½ oz firm tofu, diced • 200ml/7fl oz apple juice • 2 tbsp sunflower oil • 2 tbsp honey
• 200ml/7fl oz soya milk • 1 tbsp cocoa powder • 50g/1¾oz dark chocolate • 2 tsp vanilla extract
• 700g/1lb 9oz cherries, pitted (500g/1lb 2oz frozen; the rest chopped and set aside)

1 Put the tofu, apple juice, sunflower oil and honey in the Vita-Mix machine and secure the 2-part lid. Select
VARIABLE speed 1. Turn the machine on and increase the speed to 10, then to HIGH. Run for 20 seconds
or until smooth. Pour the tofu mixture into a shallow freezerproof container and freeze for 4–5 hours or
until frozen. After 1 hour into the freezing time, use a knife to cut the mixture into ice-cube-sized pieces,
then continue to freeze. Wash the Vita-Mix machine.
2 Put the soya milk, cocoa powder, dark chocolate and vanilla extract in the Vita-Mix machine and secure the
2-part lid. Select VARIABLE speed 1. Turn the machine on and increase the speed to 10, then to HIGH. Run
for 10 seconds until mixed.
3 Add the frozen tofu mixture and frozen cherries and continue to run on HIGH, using the tamper to push
the ingredients into the blades. In about 30 seconds the sound of the motor will change and 4 mounds
should form in the mixture. Stop the machine, stir in the remaining cherries and serve immediately.

HEALTH BENEFITS • Energizing • Anti-ageing • High protein • High fibre • Low cholesterol
• Low saturated fat

Piña Colada Ice Cream

SERVES 4 **PREPARATION TIME:** 10 minutes, plus 4–5 hours for freezing the pineapple and coconut milk
VITA-MIX TIME: 1 minute **SERVE WITH:** Grilled pineapple wedges or tropical fruit salad
STORAGE: Put in a shallow freezerproof container and freeze for up to 3 months. Remove from the
freezer 15 minutes before serving to allow it to soften slightly.
IF USING THE 32oz CONTAINER: Halve the quantities.

250ml/9fl oz coconut cream • 2 tbsp coconut-flavoured liqueur • 2 tbsp honey • 1 ripe pineapple,
peeled, cut into chunks and frozen • 125ml/4fl oz coconut milk, frozen in an ice-cube tray
• mint leaves, to decorate

1 Put all the ingredients, except the mint, in the Vita-Mix machine in the order listed and secure the 2-part
lid. Select VARIABLE speed 1. Turn the machine on and increase the speed to 10, then to HIGH, using the
tamper to push the ingredients into the blades.
2 In 40 seconds to 1 minute, the sound of the motor will change and 4 mounds should form in the mixture.
Stop the machine. Serve immediately, decorated with mint leaves.

HEALTH BENEFITS • Energizing • Immune boosting • Anti-ageing • Low cholesterol

Raspberry & Rosewater Ice Cream

SERVES 4 **PREPARATION TIME:** 5 minutes **VITA-MIX TIME:** 30 seconds
SERVE WITH: Fresh raspberries and berry coulis (see Lemon Ricotta Cheesecake, page 145)
STORAGE: Put in a shallow freezerproof container and freeze for up to 3 months. Remove from
the freezer 15 minutes before serving to allow it to soften slightly.
IF USING THE 32oz CONTAINER: Halve the quantities.

250ml/9fl oz raspberry yogurt • 3 tbsp icing sugar • 1 tbsp rosewater • 300g/10½oz frozen raspberries

1 Put the ingredients in the Vita-Mix machine in the order listed and secure the 2-part lid. Select VARIABLE
speed 1. Turn the machine on and increase the speed to 10, then to HIGH, using the tamper to push the
ingredients into the blades.

2 In about 30 seconds, the sound of the motor will change and 4 mounds should form in the mixture. Stop
the machine and serve immediately.

HEALTH BENEFITS • Energizing • Immune boosting • Stress-busting • High fibre • Low cholesterol
• Low saturated fat • Low calorie • Low kilojoule

Peach & Amaretto Gelato

SERVES 4 **PREPARATION TIME:** 3 minutes, plus 4–5 hours for freezing the peach slices
VITA-MIX TIME: 50 seconds **STORAGE:** Put in a shallow freezerproof container and freeze for
up to 3 months. Remove from the freezer 15 minutes before serving to allow it to soften slightly.
IF USING THE 32oz CONTAINER: Halve the quantities.

250ml/9fl oz single cream • 450g/1lb peach slices, frozen • 2 tbsp clear honey • 2 tsp Amaretto liqueur

1 Put the ingredients in the Vita-Mix machine in the order listed and secure the 2-part lid. Select VARIABLE
speed 1. Turn the machine on and increase the speed to 10, then to HIGH. Use the tamper through the lid
to press the peaches into the blades while running.

2 In about 30–50 seconds, the sound of the motor will change and 4 mounds should form in the mixture.
Stop the machine and serve immediately.

HEALTH BENEFITS • Energizing

Make this: dairy-free by using soya cream instead of single cream.

Chocolate & Cookies Ice Cream

SERVES 4 **PREPARATION TIME:** 5 minutes, plus 4–5 hours for freezing the bananas
VITA-MIX TIME: 32 seconds **SERVE WITH:** Chocolate Sauce (see page 25) **STORAGE:** Put in a shallow freezerproof container and freeze for up to 3 months. Remove from the freezer 15 minutes before serving to allow it to soften slightly. **IF USING THE 32oz CONTAINER:** Halve the quantities.

3 chocolate chip cookies • 240ml/8fl oz chocolate milk • 4 tbsp honey • 2 tbsp cocoa powder • 2 tbsp milk powder • 2 bananas, frozen • 30 ice cubes

1 Put the cookies in the Vita-Mix machine and secure the 2-part lid. Select VARIABLE speed 2 and pulse on and off 1–2 times to break up the cookies into small pieces. Transfer to a bowl and set aside. Wash the Vita-Mix machine.
2 Put the remaining ingredients in the Vita-Mix machine in the order listed. Secure the 2-part lid, select VARIABLE speed 1 and turn the machine on. Increase the speed to 10, then to HIGH, using the tamper to push the ingredients into the blades. In about 30 seconds the sound of the motor will change and 4 mounds should form in the mixture. Stop the machine, stir in the cookies and serve immediately.

HEALTH BENEFITS • Energizing

Make this: *wheat- and gluten-free by using chocolate chips instead of cookies.*

Strawberry & Apricot Frozen Yogurt

SERVES 4 **PREPARATION TIME:** 5 minutes, plus 4–5 hours for freezing the apricots
VITA-MIX TIME: 1 minute **STORAGE:** Put in a shallow freezerproof container and freeze for
up to 3 months. Remove from the freezer 1 hour before serving to allow it to soften slightly.
IF USING THE 32oz CONTAINER: Halve the quantities.

150ml/5fl oz natural yogurt • 2 tbsp sugar • 250g/9oz apricots, pitted, chopped and frozen
• 125g/4½oz frozen strawberries

1 Put the ingredients in the Vita-Mix machine in the order listed and secure the 2-part lid. Select VARIABLE
   speed 1. Turn the machine on and increase the speed to 10, then to HIGH, using the tamper to push the
   ingredients into the blades.
2 In about 1 minute, the sound of the motor will change and 4 mounds should form in the mixture. Stop
   the machine and serve immediately.

HEALTH BENEFITS • Energizing • Detoxifying • Immune-boosting • Weight-shifting • High fibre
• Low cholesterol • Low saturated fat • Low calorie • Low kilojoule

Make this: *dairy-free by using soya yogurt instead of natural yogurt.*

Mocha Hazelnut Semifreddo

SERVES 4 **PREPARATION TIME:** 5 minutes, plus 4–5 hours for freezing the cream
VITA-MIX TIME: 10–15 seconds **COOKING TIME:** 3 minutes
STORAGE: Put in a shallow freezerproof container and freeze for up to 3 months. Remove
from the freezer 30 minutes before serving to allow it to soften slightly.
IF USING THE 32oz CONTAINER: Halve the quantities.

70g/2¼oz blanched hazelnuts • 150ml/5fl oz evaporated milk • 2–3 tbsp brown sugar
• 1 tbsp instant coffee granules • 2 tsp vanilla extract • 500ml/17fl oz single cream, frozen
in an ice-cube tray

1 Put the hazelnuts in a heavy-based saucepan over a medium heat and cook for 3 minutes, stirring
   frequently, until lightly toasted.
2 Put the hazelnuts, evaporated milk, brown sugar, coffee granules, vanilla extract and frozen cream
   cubes in the Vita-Mix machine in that order and secure the 2-part lid. Select VARIABLE speed 1, turn
   the machine on and increase the speed to 10, then to HIGH, using the tamper to push the ingredients
   into the blades.
3 In about 10–15 seconds, the sound of the motor will change and 4 mounds should form in the mixture.
   Stop the machine and serve immediately.

HEALTH BENEFITS • Energizing • High protein

Papaya & Coconut Cream

SERVES 4 **PREPARATION TIME:** 10 minutes, plus 1 hour chilling
VITA-MIX TIME: 35 seconds **SERVE WITH:** Grated dark chocolate sprinkled on top
STORAGE: Can be kept in the fridge for up to 2 days.
IF USING THE 32oz CONTAINER: Halve the quantities.

500g/1lb 2oz firm tofu, diced • 200ml/7fl oz orange juice • 5cm/2in piece root ginger, peeled
• 3 tbsp clear honey • 2 papayas, peeled and deseeded • 50g/1¾oz coconut, broken into pieces
• 50g/1¾oz creamed coconut (optional)

1 Put the tofu, orange juice, ginger and honey in the Vita-Mix machine and secure the 2-part lid. Select VARIABLE speed 1. Turn the machine on and increase the speed to 10, then to HIGH. Run for 20 seconds or until smooth and creamy.
2 Remove the lid plug and add the papaya, coconut and creamed coconut, if using. Run for a further 15 seconds until well combined. Divide into four dessert glasses, cover and chill for 1 hour, then serve.

HEALTH BENEFITS • Energizing • Detoxifying • Immune-boosting • Anti-ageing • Stress-busting
• High protein • High fibre • Low cholesterol

Make this: *vegan by using sugar or brown rice syrup instead of honey.*

Chocolate & Chestnut Pudding

SERVES 4 **PREPARATION TIME:** 6 minutes, plus 1 hour chilling **VITA-MIX TIME:** 1 minute
STORAGE: Can be kept in the fridge for up to 2 days.

240g/8½oz cooked and peeled chestnuts • 4 dates, pitted • 420ml/14½fl oz double cream
• 1 tbsp sugar or honey • 50g/1¾oz dark chocolate, plus shavings for decoration • 1 tbsp cocoa powder
• 1 tsp vanilla extract • zest of 1 orange

1 Put all the ingredients in the Vita-Mix machine in the order listed and secure the 2-part lid. Select VARIABLE speed 6 and run for 1 minute or until smooth and creamy, using the tamper to push the chestnuts into the blades if necessary.
2 Spoon the mixture into four dessert glasses and chill for 1 hour until set. Serve sprinkled with dark chocolate shavings.

HEALTH BENEFITS • Energizing • High fibre

Mango Sorbet

SERVES 4 **PREPARATION TIME:** 12 minutes, plus 4–5 hours for freezing the mangoes
VITA-MIX TIME: 30 seconds **STORAGE:** Put in a shallow freezerproof container and freeze
for up to 3 months. Remove from the freezer 1 hour before serving to allow it to soften slightly.
IF USING THE 32oz CONTAINER: Halve the quantities.

4 mangoes, peeled and chopped (2 frozen; 2 at room temperature) • 5 tbsp sugar • 14 ice cubes

1 Put the 2 unfrozen mangoes in the Vita-Mix machine. Add the sugar, frozen mangoes and ice cubes
  in that order and secure the 2-part lid. Select VARIABLE speed 1. Turn the machine on and increase
  the speed to 10, then to HIGH, using the tamper to push the ingredients into the blades while running.
2 In about 30 seconds, the sound of the motor will change and 4 mounds should form in the mixture.
  Stop the machine and serve immediately.

HEALTH BENEFITS • Energizing • Weight-shifting • High fibre • Low cholesterol • Low saturated fat
• Low calorie • Low kilojoule

Make this: *sugar-free by omitting the sugar.*

Blackcurrant Tofu Cheesecake

MAKES 20cm/8in cheesecake **PREPARATION TIME:** 10 minutes, plus 1 hour chilling
VITA-MIX TIME: 2 minutes **COOKING TIME:** 47 minutes
STORAGE: Leftovers will keep in the fridge for 3–4 days.
NOT SUITABLE FOR THE 32oz CONTAINER.

300g/10½oz granola • 300ml/10½fl oz pineapple juice • 500g/1lb 2oz firm tofu, diced
• 60ml/2fl oz sunflower oil • 100ml/3½fl oz clear honey • 2 tsp vanilla extract
• 250g/9oz blackcurrant jam

1 Preheat the oven to 190°C/375°F/Gas 5. Put the granola cereal and 100ml/3½fl oz of the pineapple juice in the Vita-Mix machine and secure the 2-part lid. Select VARIABLE speed 5 and run for 1 minute or until well mixed. Spoon the mixture into the base of a 20cm/8in springform pan, then bake for 12 minutes or until golden brown. Wash the Vita-Mix machine.
2 Put the remaining pineapple juice in the Vita-Mix machine, along with the tofu, sunflower oil, honey and vanilla extract and secure the 2-part lid. Select VARIABLE speed 1. Turn the machine on and increase the speed to 10, then to HIGH. Run for 1 minute or until smooth and creamy.
3 Pour the mixture over the granola base and bake for a further 30–35 minutes or until set. Remove from the oven and leave to cool completely, then spread the jam over the top. Chill for 1 hour, then serve.

HEALTH BENEFITS • Energizing • Immune-boosting • Anti-ageing • Stress-busting • High protein • High fibre • Low cholesterol • Low saturated fat

Make this: *vegan by using brown rice syrup instead of honey.*

Blueberry Crème Anglaise Tart

SERVES 6 **PREPARATION TIME:** 15 minutes, plus 20 minutes chilling
VITA-MIX TIME: 4 minutes **COOKING TIME:** 55 minutes
STORAGE: Make in advance and keep in the fridge for up to 2 days.

300g/10½oz plain flour, plus extra for rolling the dough • 150g/5½oz butter • 3 tbsp caster sugar
• 225g/8oz blueberries
Filling: 125ml/4fl oz full-fat milk • 150ml/5fl oz double cream • 3 eggs • 75g/2½oz caster sugar

1 Preheat the oven to 200°C/400°F/Gas 6. Put the flour in a bowl. Using your fingertips, rub in the butter until the mixture resembles fine breadcrumbs. Add the sugar and 1–2 tablespoons water and mix to form a soft dough. Knead lightly, then wrap in cling film and chill for 20 minutes.
2 On a lightly floured surface, roll out the pastry so that it is large enough to line a 23cm/9in flan tin. Line the pastry case with greaseproof paper and cover it with baking beans. Bake for 20 minutes, removing the beans and paper after 15 minutes. Remove from the oven and leave to cool slightly. Reduce the oven temperature to 180°C/350°F/Gas 4.
3 To make the filling, put the milk in a pan and heat over a medium heat for 2 minutes, stirring occasionally, until hot. Transfer the milk to the Vita-Mix and add the cream, eggs and sugar. Secure the 2-part lid and select VARIABLE speed 1. Turn the machine on and increase the speed to 10, then to HIGH. Run for 4 minutes until hot and slightly thickened.
4 Scatter the blueberries into the pastry case tin and pour over the custard filling. Bake for 35 minutes until just set and golden brown. Leave to cool, then serve.

HEALTH BENEFITS • Energizing

Lemon Ricotta Cheesecake

MAKES 23cm/9in cheesecake **PREPARATION TIME:** 10 minutes, plus 45 minutes cooling
VITA-MIX TIME: 20 seconds **COOKING TIME:** 40 minutes
STORAGE: Leftovers will keep in the fridge for 3–4 days. The berry coulis can be frozen for up to 1 month.
Defrost in the fridge overnight before serving. **NOT SUITABLE FOR THE 32oz CONTAINER.**

225g/8oz oat biscuits • 125g/4½oz unsalted butter, melted, plus extra for greasing • 2 tbsp honey
• 500g/1lb 2oz ricotta cheese • zest of 3 lemons • 4 tbsp lemon juice • 80g/2¾oz caster sugar
• 3 egg yolks • 2 tbsp cornflour
Coulis: 25g/1oz icing sugar • 500g/1lb 2oz mixed berries, such as raspberries and strawberries

1 Preheat the oven to 180°C/350°F/Gas 4 and lightly grease a 23cm/9in springform cake tin. Put the
   biscuits in the Vita-Mix machine and secure the 2-part lid. Select VARIABLE speed 3 and run for a few
   seconds until crumbs form, using the tamper to push the biscuits into the blades if necessary. Turn off
   the machine, add the melted butter and honey and pulse on and off a few times to mix thoroughly.
   Spoon the biscuit mixture into the tin and press down into the base. Wash the Vita-Mix machine.
2 Put the ricotta cheese, lemon zest, lemon juice, sugar, egg yolks and cornflour in the Vita-Mix machine
   and secure the 2-part lid. Select VARIABLE speed 1. Turn the machine on and increase the speed to 10,
   then to HIGH. Run for 10 seconds or until well blended. Pour the lemon filling into the prepared tin
   and bake for 35–40 minutes until firm. Turn off the oven and leave the cheesecake to cool in the oven
   for 45 minutes.
3 To make the coulis, put the sugar and 250g/9oz of the berries in the Vita-Mix machine and secure the
   2-part lid. Select VARIABLE speed 1. Turn the machine on and increase the speed to 10, then to HIGH.
   Run for 5–6 seconds until smooth. Strain the coulis through a sieve to remove any pips.
4 To serve, cut the cheesecake into slices and drizzle over the berry coulis. Serve with the remaining berries.

HEALTH BENEFITS • Energizing • High protein

Make this: dairy-free by using silken tofu instead of ricotta cheese in the filling and soya margarine
instead of butter in the biscuit base.

Fruit Kebabs with Orange
& Passionfruit Sauce

SERVES 4 **PREPARATION TIME:** 20 minutes **VITA-MIX TIME:** 15 seconds
COOKING TIME: 11 minutes **SERVE WITH:** Vanilla Ice Cream (see page 136) drizzled with any
remaining sauce **STORAGE:** The kebabs are best served straight away, although the sauce can
be made in advance and kept in the fridge for up to 3 days.

400g/14oz strawberries, hulled • 3 kiwi fruit, peeled and cut into 2.5cm/1in cubes • ½ pineapple,
peeled and cut into 2.5cm/1in cubes • 3 bananas, peeled and cut into 2.5cm/1in cubes
Sauce 4 passionfruit • 2 oranges, peeled and quartered • 1 tbsp lime juice • 2 tbsp clear honey

1 Preheat the grill to medium. If using wooden skewers, soak them in cold water for 30 minutes before
   using. Arrange the fruit alternately on 8 skewers and put them on a baking sheet.
2 To make the sauce, put a fine sieve over a bowl. Cut the passionfruit in half and scoop out the pulp
   into the sieve, then press it through the sieve, using the back of a teaspoon. Discard the seeds.
3 Put the passionfruit juice, oranges, lime juice and honey in the Vita-Mix machine and secure the
   2-part lid. Select VARIABLE speed 1. Turn the machine on and increase the speed to 10, then to HIGH.
   Run for 15 seconds or until smooth. Transfer the mixture to a small saucepan. Bring to the boil over
   a medium-high heat, then reduce the heat to low and simmer for 4–5 minutes or until thick.
4 Brush the kebabs with the sauce and grill for 6 minutes, turning frequently, until lightly browned.
   Serve immediately, drizzled with any remaining sauce.

HEALTH BENEFITS • Energizing • Detoxifying • Immune-boosting • Anti-ageing • Stress-busting
• Weight-shifting • High fibre • Low cholesterol • Low saturated fat • Low calorie • Low kilojoule

Cherry & Almond Clafoutis

SERVES 4–6 **PREPARATION TIME:** 5 minutes **VITA-MIX TIME:** 1 minute **COOKING TIME:** 40 minutes
STORAGE: Leftovers will keep in the fridge for up to 2 days.

butter, for greasing • 400g/14oz cherries, pitted • 2 tbsp Morello cherry jam • 2 tbsp ground almonds
Batter: 3 eggs • 50g/1¾oz plain flour • 300ml/10½fl oz double cream • 2 tbsp caster sugar
• a pinch cinnamon • icing sugar, for dusting

1 Preheat the oven to 180°C/350°C/Gas 4 and lightly grease a shallow 20cm/8in baking dish. Put the
cherries, jam and 1 tablespoon water in a small saucepan over a medium-low heat and simmer gently for
1–2 minutes, stirring continuously, until the jam melts and the cherries soften slightly. Transfer the mixture
to the baking dish and mix in the almonds.
2 Put the ingredients for the batter in the Vita-Mix machine and secure the 2-part lid. Select VARIABLE speed
1. Turn the machine on and increase the speed to 10, then to HIGH. Run for 1 minute until thoroughly
combined. Leave to stand for a 2–3 minutes.
3 Pour the batter over the cherries and bake for 30–35 minutes until firm. Dust with a little icing sugar
and serve hot.

HEALTH BENEFITS • Energizing

Make this: dairy-free by using soya milk or soya cream instead of double cream and oil instead
of butter for greasing the baking dish.

Baked Stuffed Peaches

SERVES 4 **PREPARATION TIME:** 10 minutes **VITA-MIX TIME:** 10 seconds **COOKING TIME:** 45 minutes
SERVE WITH: Greek yogurt **STORAGE:** These will keep in the fridge for up to 1 day.

50g/1¾oz unsalted butter, melted, plus extra for greasing • 4 large peaches, halved and pitted
• 50g/1¾oz pecan nuts • 250g/9oz ginger biscuits or cookies • 2 tbsp honey

1 Preheat the oven to 180°C/350°F/Gas 4 and lightly grease a baking dish. Using a teaspoon, scoop
out a little of the peach flesh to enlarge the hollows and put it in the Vita-Mix machine.
2 Add the melted butter, pecan nuts, biscuits and honey and secure the 2-part lid. Select VARIABLE speed 5
and pulse on and off for 10 seconds or until the mixture is crushed and well mixed.
3 Fill the peach hollows with the stuffing, then arrange the peaches in the baking dish and add a few
tablespoons of water to the base. Bake for 40–45 minutes or until the peaches are tender and the topping
is golden. Serve warm.

HEALTH BENEFITS • Energizing • High fibre

Pumpkin Pie

SERVES 6 **PREPARATION TIME:** 15 minutes, plus 20 minutes chilling **VITA-MIX TIME:** 30 seconds
COOKING TIME: 1 hour 40 minutes **SERVE WITH:** Crème fraîche or whipped cream
STORAGE: Leftovers will keep in the fridge for up to 2 days.

450g/1lb pumpkin, peeled and diced • 1 tbsp olive oil • 125g/4½oz soft brown sugar • 2 eggs
• 1 tsp vanilla extract • 1 tsp cinnamon • 1 tsp ground nutmeg • 300ml/10½fl oz double cream
Pastry: 300g/10½oz plain flour • 150g/5½oz butter • 3 tbsp caster sugar

1 Preheat the oven to 200°C/400°F/Gas 6. To make the pastry, put the flour in a bowl and, using
   your fingertips, rub in the butter until the mixture resembles fine breadcrumbs. Add the sugar and
   1–2 tablespoons water and work together to form a soft dough. Knead lightly, then wrap in cling film
   and chill for 20 minutes.
2 Put the pumpkin in a large bowl, drizzle over the oil and toss well, then transfer to a roasting tin. Bake
   for 30 minutes until soft. Remove from the oven and leave to cool slightly, then put in a sieve over a bowl
   to drain off the excess liquid.
3 On a lightly floured surface, roll out the pastry so that it is large enough to line a deep 23cm/9in pie dish.
   Line the pastry case with baking parchment and cover with baking beans. Bake in the oven for 20 minutes,
   removing the beans and paper after 15 minutes. Remove from the oven and leave to cool slightly.
4 Put the pumpkin and the remaining ingredients in the Vita-Mix machine and secure the 2-part lid. Select
   VARIABLE speed 1. Turn the machine on and increase the speed to 10, then to HIGH. Run for 30 seconds
   until the mixture is thoroughly combined.
5 Pour the filling into the pastry case and bake for 40–50 minutes until golden brown and just slightly
   wobbly in the centre. Cover with foil if the crust gets too brown during cooking. Remove from the oven
   and leave to cool slightly, then serve.

HEALTH BENEFITS • Energizing • High fibre

Baked Bananas with Chocolate Fudge Sauce

SERVES 4 **PREPARATION TIME:** 5 minutes **VITA-MIX TIME:** 4 minutes **COOKING TIME:** 15 minutes
STORAGE: The fudge sauce will keep in the fridge for up to 2 days. The sauce will also freeze well for
up to 1 month. Defrost in the fridge then warm gently in the Vita-Mix machine or a saucepan to serve.

4 bananas, peeled • 2 tbsp orange juice • 3 tbsp flaked almonds
Sauce 125ml/4fl oz double cream • 50g/1¾oz butter • 100g/3½oz light soft brown sugar
• 50g/1¾oz dark chocolate • 2 tbsp maple syrup

1 Preheat the oven to 200°C/400°F/Gas 6. Heat the cream over a medium heat until warm and transfer
   to the Vita-Mix machine. Add the remaining ingredients for the sauce, secure the 2-part lid and select
   VARIABLE speed 1. Turn the machine on and increase the speed to 10, then to HIGH. Run for 3–4 minutes
   until hot and thick. Meanwhile, cut the bananas in half lengthways and put each one on a sheet of foil.
2 Sprinkle the orange juice and almonds over the bananas and wrap in the foil. Transfer to a baking sheet
   and bake for 15 minutes until soft, then spoon the sauce over the bananas and serve hot.

HEALTH BENEFITS • Energizing • High fibre

Make this: *dairy-free by using dairy-free chocolate, soya cream and soya margarine.*

Raspberry & Plum Crumble

SERVES 4 **PREPARATION TIME:** 15 minutes **VITA-MIX TIME:** 18 seconds
COOKING TIME: 20 minutes **SERVE WITH:** Vanilla Ice Cream (see page 136), cream or natural yogurt
STORAGE: Leftovers will keep in the fridge for up to 2 days.

5 plums, halved and pitted • 100g/3½oz raspberries • 2 tbsp raspberry jam • 2 tbsp sugar
Crumble 140g/5oz rolled oats • 25g/1oz walnuts • 2 tbsp demerara sugar • a pinch ground ginger
• a pinch cinnamon • 50g/1¾oz unsalted butter

1 Preheat the oven to 190°C/375°F/Gas 5. Put the plums, raspberries, jam and sugar in the Vita-Mix
  machine and secure the 2-part lid. Select VARIABLE speed 1 and run for 10 seconds or until almost
  smooth, using the tamper to push the fruit into the blades. Transfer to a 20cm/8in baking dish and
  set aside. Wash the Vita-Mix machine.
2 To make the crumble, put the oats, walnuts, sugar, ginger and cinnamon in the Vita-Mix machine
  and secure the 2-part lid. Select VARIABLE speed 1 and run for 6–8 seconds or until well mixed.
  Transfer to a bowl and, using your fingertips, rub in the butter to make a crumble mixture, then
  spread it over the fruit.
3 Bake for 20 minutes or until golden brown, then serve.

HEALTH BENEFITS • Energizing • Immune-boosting • High fibre

Make this: *gluten-free by using millet flakes instead of oats. Make this dairy-free by using vegetable
margarine instead of butter.*

Special Occasions

Baked Scallops with Capers & Lemon–Oregano Butter

Fettuccine with Pumpkin & Asparagus in a Creamy Provençal Sauce

SERVES 4 **PREPARATION TIME:** 20 minutes **VITA-MIX TIME:** 40 seconds
COOKING TIME: 1 hour **SERVE WITH:** A leafy green salad and roasted mixed peppers
STORAGE: Best served straight away, although the sauce can be made in advance and kept in the fridge for up to 2 days.

½ pumpkin, peeled, deseeded and diced • 1 tsp paprika • 1 tbsp olive oil • 200g/7oz asparagus, chopped • 400g/14oz fettuccine

Sauce 500g/1lb 2oz tomatoes, halved • 2 red peppers, quartered and deseeded • 2 tbsp olive oil • 2 carrots, peeled and quartered • ½ onion • 2 garlic cloves • 2 basil sprigs • ¼ tsp dried oregano • a pinch dried thyme • a pinch dried rosemary • 1 tsp lemon juice • 1 small handful flat-leaf parsley • salt and freshly ground black pepper

1 Preheat the oven to 200°C/400°F/Gas 6. To make the sauce, put the tomatoes and red peppers in a baking dish, drizzle over the oil and mix well. Bake for 20 minutes, stirring occasionally, until tender. Remove from the oven and lower the temperature to 190°C/375°F/Gas 5.
2 Transfer the tomatoes and peppers to the Vita-Mix and add the carrots, onion, garlic, basil, dried herbs and lemon juice. Season with salt and pepper and secure the 2-part lid. Select VARIABLE speed 5 and run for 30 seconds until the mixture is well combined. Add the parsley and pulse on and off a few times until finely chopped.
3 Put the pumpkin in a baking dish and sprinkle the paprika over, then mix in the olive oil. Bake for 40 minutes until tender.
4 Bring a large pan of water to the boil and cook the fettuccine according to the packet instructions until al dente, then drain and transfer to a large bowl. Meanwhile, put the chopped asparagus in a steamer and cook for 5 minutes until tender.
5 Transfer the sauce to a pan and heat through over a medium heat, then mix it into the fettuccine, tossing well to coat. Mix in the asparagus and pumpkin and serve immediately.

HEALTH BENEFITS • Energizing • Immune-boosting • Anti-ageing • Stress-busting • High fibre • Low cholesterol • Low saturated fat

Make this: gluten- and wheat-free by using rice or buckwheat noodles instead of fettuccini. Make this citrus free by omitting the lemon juice.

Sweet Potato & Spinach Crêpes with Cashew Nut Sauce

SERVES 4 **PREPARATION TIME:** 15 minutes **VITA-MIX TIME:** 1 minute
COOKING TIME: 35 minutes **SERVE WITH:** Ratatouille (see page 94) and a watercress or mixed bean salad **STORAGE:** Best served straight away, although the sauce can be made in advance and kept in the fridge for up to 2 days.

Sauce 200g/7oz cashew nuts • 250ml/9fl oz vegetable stock • 1 shallot • 1 small garlic clove • 1 tsp dried mixed herbs • 1 tsp paprika • salt and freshly ground black pepper
Crêpes 125g/4½oz plain flour • a pinch salt • 2 eggs • 200ml/7fl oz full-fat milk • 1 small handful flat-leaf parsley • 6 chives • 3–5 tbsp sunflower oil
Filling 2 tbsp olive oil • 1 onion, chopped • 1 tbsp mustard seeds • 800g/1lb 12oz sweet potatoes, peeled and diced • 100ml/3½fl oz vegetable stock • 200g/7oz baby spinach, chopped

1 Put the ingredients for the sauce in the Vita-Mix machine, season with salt and pepper and secure the 2-part lid. Select VARIABLE speed 5 and run for 30 seconds or until smooth and creamy. Transfer to a bowl and set aside. Wash the Vita-Mix machine.
2 To make the crêpe batter, put the flour, salt, eggs, milk, parsley, chives and 2 tablespoons of the sunflower oil in the Vita-Mix machine. Add 100ml/3½fl oz water and secure the 2-part lid. Select VARIABLE speed 5 and run for 30 seconds or until smooth and well combined. Set aside while you make the filling.
3 For the filling, heat the oil in a large pan over a medium heat. Add the onion and mustard seeds and fry for 2–3 minutes, stirring occasionally, until the onion is softened. Add the sweet potatoes and vegetable stock and bring to the boil, then reduce the heat to low and simmer for 15–20 minutes or until the sweet potatoes are almost soft. Add the spinach and cook for a further 3–4 minutes until the spinach has wilted and the potatoes are cooked through. Mix well to combine, taking care not to over-mix or the potatoes will become mushy.
4 Stir the cashew nut sauce into the vegetable filling and mix gently.
5 To make the crêpes, heat 1 tablespoon of the remaining oil in a large non-stick frying pan over a medium heat. Pour in a ladleful of batter and swirl it around until it thinly covers the base of the pan. Cook for 1 minute on each side until golden. Transfer to a plate and cover with another plate to keep warm. Repeat with the remaining batter to make 4 crêpes, adding more oil to the pan as needed.
6 Spread half of each crêpe with the filling and fold over, then serve.

HEALTH BENEFITS • Energizing • Immune-boosting • Stress-Busting • High protein • Low cholesterol • Low saturated fat

Make this: *seed-free by using olive oil instead of sunflower oil.*

Vegetarian Moussaka

SERVES 6 **PREPARATION TIME:** 15 minutes **VITA-MIX TIME:** 1 minute 40 seconds
COOKING TIME: 1 hour 45 minutes **SERVE WITH:** A leafy green salad
STORAGE: Leftovers will keep in the fridge for up to 3 days.

3–4 tbsp olive oil • 1 onion, chopped • 2 celery sticks, chopped • 1 courgette, trimmed and chopped
• 250g/9oz brown lentils • 600ml/21fl oz vegetable stock • 6 tomatoes, halved • 1 tbsp sun-dried
tomato paste • 1 garlic clove • 1 tsp dried oregano • 1 tsp tamari • 1 handful flat-leaf parsley
• 2 aubergines, thinly sliced • 250ml/9fl oz Greek yogurt • 1 egg • 100g/3½oz feta cheese • a pinch
nutmeg • 50g/1¾oz Cheddar cheese, grated • freshly ground black pepper

1 Preheat the oven to 180°C/350°F/Gas 4 and the grill to low. Heat 1 tablespoon of the oil over a medium
heat and add the onion. Cook for 3 minutes, stirring occasionally, until soft, then add the celery and
courgette and cook for a further 2 minutes. Add the lentils and vegetable stock and bring to the boil,
then reduce the heat to low and simmer, covered, for 50 minutes until the lentils are soft.
2 Meanwhile, put the tomatoes, sun-dried tomato paste, garlic, oregano, tamari and 1 tablespoon of the
oil in the Vita-Mix machine and secure the 2-part lid. Select VARIABLE speed 1. Turn the machine on and
increase the speed to 10, then to HIGH. Run for 1 minute or until smooth. Remove the lid plug and add
the parsley. Replace the plug and pulse on and off until finely chopped.
3 Brush the aubergine slices with the remaining olive oil, put them on a baking sheet and grill for 6 minutes
on each side or until softened.
4 When the lentils have finished cooking, stir in the tomato mixture and heat through. Transfer the lentils
to a 30 x 20cm/12 x 8in baking dish and layer the aubergines on top. Wash the Vita-Mix machine.
5 Put the yogurt, egg, feta and nutmeg in the Vita-Mix machine and season with pepper. Secure the 2-part
lid and select VARIABLE speed 1. Turn the machine on and increase the speed to 10, then to HIGH. Run
for 30 seconds until well mixed, then pour the mixture over the aubergines. Top with the Cheddar cheese
and bake for 40 minutes until golden, then serve.

HEALTH BENEFITS • Energizing • Immune-boosting • Stress-busting • High protein • High fibre

Carrot & Chestnut Terrine

SERVES 4–6 **PREPARATION TIME:** 15 minutes **VITA-MIX TIME:** 22 seconds
COOKING TIME: 1 hour 10 minutes **STORAGE:** This will keep in the fridge for up to 3 days.

butter, for greasing
Chestnut layer 1 onion • 1 garlic clove • 1 tbsp olive oil • 125g/4½oz bread • 175g/6oz cooked chestnuts
• 1 tbsp tamari • 2 flat-leaf parsley sprigs • 2 tomatoes • 60g/2¼oz cranberries • 2 eggs, beaten
• salt and freshly ground black pepper
Carrot layer 3 large carrots, peeled and sliced • 1 handful chives • 50g/1¾oz cream cheese • 1 egg

1 Preheat the oven to 180°C/350°F/Gas 4. Grease a 450g/1lb loaf tin with butter and line it with baking
parchment. To make the chestnut layer, put the onion and garlic in the Vita-Mix machine and secure the
2-part lid. Select VARIABLE speed 1 and run for 4–5 seconds until finely chopped. Heat the oil in a frying
pan over a medium-high heat, add the onion and garlic and cook for 2 minutes, stirring occasionally, until
softened, then transfer to a bowl. Wash the Vita-Mix machine.
2 Put the bread in the Vita-Mix machine and secure the 2-part lid. Select VARIABLE speed 1 and run for
5–6 seconds until breadcrumbs form. Add to the bowl with the onion.
3 Put the chestnuts, tamari, parsley and tomatoes in the Vita-Mix machine and season with salt and pepper.
Select VARIABLE speed 1 and run for 3–4 seconds until coarsely chopped, using the tamper to press the
mixture into the blades. Add the mixture to the breadcrumbs, then add the cranberries and eggs. Season
with salt and pepper and mix well. Wash the Vita-Mix machine.
4 Put all the ingredients for the carrot layer in the Vita-Mix machine and secure the 2-part lid. Select
VARIABLE speed 1. Turn the machine on and increase to speed 6. Run for 6–7 seconds until smooth.
5 Spoon half the chestnut mixture into the tin and press down firmly. Spoon over the carrot mixture, then
top with the remaining chestnut mixture. Bake for 1 hour to 1 hour 10 minutes until firm to the touch
and golden brown. Leave to cool in the tin before turning out, then slice and serve.

HEALTH BENEFITS • Energizing • Immune-boosting • Stress-busting • High fibre • High protein

Japanese Prawn & Soy Dumplings

SERVES 4 **PREPARATION TIME:** 15 minutes **VITA-MIX TIME:** 5 seconds
COOKING TIME: 16 minutes **SERVE WITH:** Sweet Chilli Sauce (see page 23) or Quick Miso Fish Soup (see page 68) **STORAGE:** Best served straight away. The filling can be prepared 1 day in advance and kept in the fridge.

100g/3½oz cooked peeled prawns • 60g/2¼oz tinned water chestnuts, drained • 1cm/½in piece root ginger, peeled • 1 garlic clove • 2 tsp cornflour • 2 tsp tamari, plus extra for dipping • 1 tsp sesame oil • 16 wonton wrappers • 1 tbsp olive oil

1 Put the prawns, water chestnuts, ginger and garlic in the Vita-Mix machine and secure the 2-part lid. Select VARIABLE speed 1 and run for 4–5 seconds until finely minced. Scrape down the mixture from the sides of the container to ensure it is evenly chopped. Transfer to a bowl and mix in the cornflour, tamari and sesame oil.
2 Put 1 teaspoon of the mixture in the centre of each wonton wrapper. Moisten the edges with water and fold over to create a triangle shape, then press the edges to seal tightly. Alternatively, you can pinch the edges to form a pouch.
3 Bring a large pan of water to the boil and add the olive oil. Drop 4 dumplings into the pan and cook for 4 minutes until they rise to the surface. Remove with a slotted spoon and repeat with the remaining dumplings. Serve immediately with tamari for dipping.

HEALTH BENEFITS • Energizing • Immune-boosting

Lobster Spaghetti

SERVES 4 **PREPARATION TIME:** 10 minutes **VITA-MIX TIME:** 4 minutes 6 seconds
COOKING TIME: 8 minutes **SERVE WITH:** A mixed salad
STORAGE: Leftovers will keep in the fridge until the following day.

1 cooked lobster • 1 red onion • 300g/10½oz spaghetti • 1 red chilli, deseeded • 2 garlic cloves
• 6 large plum tomatoes, seeds removed • 2 tbsp Pernod • 4 tbsp crème fraîche • 2 tbsp olive oil
• 2 tbsp chopped basil leaves • salt and freshly ground black pepper

1 Remove the meat from the lobster and cut into large chunks.
2 Put the onion in the Vita-Mix machine and secure the 2-part lid. Select VARIABLE speed 1 and run
  for 5–6 seconds until finely chopped. Transfer to a bowl and set aside. Wash the Vita-Mix machine.
3 Bring a large pan of water to the boil. Cook the pasta for 7–8 minutes or according to the packet
  instructions until al dente, then drain.
4 While the pasta is cooking, put the chilli, garlic, tomatoes, Pernod and crème fraîche in the Vita-Mix
  machine and secure the 2-part lid. Select VARIABLE speed 1. Turn the machine on and increase the speed
  to 10, then to HIGH. Run for 3–4 minutes until thick and steaming.
5 Heat the oil in a non-stick frying pan over a medium heat. Add the onion and cook for 2 minutes, stirring
  occasionally, until soft. Add the lobster and stir in the tomato cream sauce. Cook for a further 2 minutes,
  stirring occasionally, until the mixture thickens.
6 Add the pasta to the sauce, stir in the basil and season with salt and pepper. Serve immediately.

HEALTH BENEFITS • Energizing • Stress-busting • High protein

> **Make this:** *gluten- and wheat-free by using rice or buckwheat noodles instead of spaghetti.*

Baked Scallops with Capers & Lemon–Oregano Butter

SERVES 4 **PREPARATION TIME:** 10 minutes **VITA-MIX TIME:** 14 seconds
COOKING TIME: 4 minutes **SERVE WITH:** Spaghetti or linguine and a leafy green salad
STORAGE: The breadcrumb butter mixture can be prepared in advance and stored in the fridge
for up to 1 week or frozen for up to 1 month. Scallops are best cooked and eaten on the day they
are purchased.

12 scallops • 1 slice of bread • 70g/2½oz butter • zest of 2 lemons, plus extra to serve • juice of 1 lemon
• 4 oregano sprigs, plus extra to serve • 3 tbsp capers, rinsed • salt and freshly ground black pepper

1 Preheat the grill to medium-high. Put the scallops in a shallow baking dish and season with salt
  and pepper.
2 Put the bread in the Vita-Mix machine and secure the 2-part lid. Select VARIABLE speed 3 and run for
  2–3 seconds until fine breadcrumbs form. Transfer to a bowl and set aside.
3 Put the butter, lemon zest, lemon juice and oregano in the Vita-Mix machine and secure the 2-part lid.
  Select VARIABLE speed 4 and run for 3 seconds or until well mixed. Scrape the butter from the sides
  of the container, using a spatula, then run for a further 3 seconds to ensure it is well mixed. Remove
  the lid plug, add the breadcrumbs and run for 4–5 seconds until combined.
4 Spoon the butter mixture evenly over the scallops, then sprinkle the capers on top.
5 Grill for 4 minutes until the breadcrumbs are golden and the scallops are opaque and cooked through.
  Sprinkle with the lemon zest and oregano and serve immediately.

HEALTH BENEFITS • Energizing • Stress-busting • High protein • Low carb

Smoked Salmon Cream Parcels

SERVES 4 **PREPARATION TIME:** 10 minutes, plus 1 hour chilling
VITA-MIX TIME: 5 seconds **SERVE WITH:** A watercress salad
STORAGE: Prepare in advance and keep in the fridge for up to 2 days.

75g/2½oz cream cheese • 3 sun-dried tomatoes in oil, drained • 2 spring onions • 1 dill sprig
• a pinch cayenne pepper • 150g/5½oz smoked salmon slices • 25g/1oz smoked salmon trimmings, diced
• freshly ground black pepper

1 Put the cream cheese, sun-dried tomatoes, spring onions and dill in the Vita-Mix machine and secure
the 2-part lid. Select VARIABLE speed 1 and run for 4–5 seconds until the tomatoes and herbs are finely
chopped and the mixture is combined, using the tamper to press the mixture into the blades. Transfer
to a bowl, stir in the cayenne pepper and season with black pepper.
2 Put a sheet of cling film on a work surface. Arrange the smoked salmon slices in a rectangle measuring
about 20 x 10cm/8 x 4in, overlapping them slightly so there are no gaps.
3 Spread the cream cheese mixture over the salmon, leaving a 1–2cm/½–¾in margin around the sides.
Scatter the salmon trimmings over. Roll up the salmon lengthways into a log, using the cling film to help
you. Twist the cling film at each end to seal. Chill in the fridge for 1 hour until firm.
4 Remove the cling film, slice the salmon into 2cm/¾in slices and serve.

HEALTH BENEFITS • Energizing • High protein • Low carb

Pistachio & Herb-Crusted Salmon with Pepper Salsa

SERVES 4 **PREPARATION TIME:** 10 minutes **VITA-MIX TIME:** 20 seconds
COOKING TIME: 12 minutes **SERVE WITH:** Herbed couscous
STORAGE: Leftover salmon can be kept chilled until the following day. You can prepare the nut
topping up to 2 days in advance. Store in an airtight container in the fridge.

60g/2¼oz pistachio nuts • 1 coriander sprig • 40g/1½oz bread • 25g/1oz butter, softened
• 4 salmon fillets, about 125g/4½oz each, skinned • salt and freshly ground black pepper
Salsa 1 red chilli, deseeded • 1 handful coriander leaves • 2 spring onions • ½ red pepper, diced
• 225g/8oz tinned sweetcorn, drained • ½ mango, diced • juice of ½ lime • ½ tsp sugar

1 Preheat the oven to 200°C/400°F/Gas 6. To make the salsa, put the chilli, coriander and spring onions
in the Vita-Mix machine and secure the 2-part lid. Select VARIABLE speed 1 and run for 3–4 seconds until
finely chopped. Scrape down the mixture from the sides of the container, using a spatula, and run for
a further 3–4 seconds to ensure the mixture is evenly chopped. Transfer to a bowl and stir in the red
pepper, sweetcorn, mango, lime juice and sugar. Cover and chill until needed. Wash the Vita-Mix machine.
2 Put the pistachio nuts, coriander and bread in the Vita-Mix machine and secure the 2-part lid. Select
VARIABLE speed 1. Turn the machine on and increase the speed to 3. Run for 6–7 seconds until finely
chopped. Add the butter and run for a further 3–4 seconds until combined, then season with pepper.
3 Put the salmon on a baking sheet and pat the surface dry with kitchen paper. Season with salt and
pepper, then divide the nut mixture on top of the salmon fillets and press down firmly.
4 Bake for 12 minutes until the salmon is cooked through and the topping is light brown. Serve
with the salsa.

HEALTH BENEFITS • Energizing • Immune-boosting • Anti-ageing • Stress-busting • High protein
• High fibre • Low carb • Low cholesterol • Low saturated fat

Make this: *dairy-free by using olive oil instead of butter. Make this wheat-free by using lightly ground
porridge oats instead of breadcrumbs.*

Pan-Fried Sea Bass with Lemon & Dill Dressing

SERVES 4 **PREPARATION TIME:** 10 minutes **VITA-MIX TIME:** 2 minutes **COOKING TIME:** 7 minutes
SERVE WITH: Fennel Coleslaw in Tofu Dressing (see page 93) and baby new potatoes
STORAGE: Leftovers will keep in the fridge until the following day.

4 sea bass fillets, about 100g/3½oz each • 1 tbsp olive oil • 2 tbsp lemon juice • 1 tbsp chopped dill
• salt and freshly ground black pepper
Dressing 2 dill sprigs • 2 spring onions • 4 tbsp olive oil • 2 tsp caster sugar • juice and zest of 1 lemon
• 2 tbsp Pernod

1 Season the sea bass fillets with salt and pepper. Heat the oil in a non-stick frying pan over a high heat.
  Add the fillets skin-side down. Press down and cook for 3 minutes until the skin is crispy, then turn over
  and cook for a further 2 minutes until the flesh is opaque and cooked through. Pour over the lemon juice
  and cook over a medium heat for 1–2 minutes until bubbling.
2 Put the ingredients for the dressing in the Vita-Mix machine and secure the 2-part lid. Select VARIABLE
  speed 1. Turn the machine on and increase the speed to 10, then to HIGH. Run for 2 minutes until the
  dressing is warm. Serve the sea bass sprinkled with the dill and accompanied by the dressing.

HEALTH BENEFITS • Energizing • Weight-shifting • High protein • Low carb • Low cholesterol
• Low saturated fat

Griddled Chicken Breasts with Green Harissa

SERVES 4 **PREPARATION TIME:** 15 minutes, plus at least 1 hour marinating
VITA-MIX TIME: 15 seconds **COOKING TIME:** 14 minutes
SERVE WITH: Millet, quinoa or steamed rice and wilted spinach
STORAGE: The harissa paste will keep in the fridge for up to 1 week. Leftover chicken will keep in the
fridge for up to 2 days.

4 skinless, boneless chicken breasts, about 125g/4½oz each • 1 tbsp olive oil • 2 tbsp chopped coriander
leaves • 1 tbsp lemon juice
Harissa paste 2 green chillies, deseeded • 1 green pepper, halved and deseeded • 3 garlic cloves
• ½ tsp salt • 4 cardamom pods, seeds only • 1 tbsp cumin seeds • 1 tbsp coriander seeds
• 1 tsp black peppercorns • 4 tbsp olive oil

1 To make the harissa, put the chillies in a small bowl and cover with boiling water. Leave to soak for
  10 minutes, then drain.
2 Put the chillies and the rest of the ingredients for the harissa in the Vita-Mix machine and secure the
  2-part lid. Select VARIABLE speed 1. Turn the machine on and increase the speed to 10, then to HIGH.
  Run for 15 seconds until the mixture forms a smooth paste, using the tamper to press the ingredients into
  the blades.
3 Put the chicken breasts between 2 sheets of cling film and flatten them to about 1cm/½in thick, using
  a rolling pin. Remove the cling film and transfer the chicken to a shallow dish. Spread half the harissa paste
  over the chicken breasts, cover and leave to marinate for at least 1 hour or overnight in the fridge.
4 Heat a griddle pan over a high heat and add the oil. Add the chicken breasts with the marinade and cook
  for 6–7 minutes on each side until cooked through and the juices run clear when the thickest part of the
  meat is pierced with a sharp knife or skewer. Sprinkle with the coriander leaves and lemon juice and serve
  with the extra harissa paste if desired.

HEALTH BENEFITS • Energizing • Immune-boosting • High protein • Low cholesterol
• Low saturated fat

Thai Stir-Fried Chicken Salad

SERVES 4 **PREPARATION TIME:** 10 minutes, plus 30 minutes marinating **VITA-MIX TIME:** 19 seconds
COOKING TIME: 7 minutes **SERVE WITH:** Steamed rice or rice noodles
STORAGE: Leftovers will keep in the fridge for up to 2 days.

3 skinless, boneless chicken breasts, about 135g/4¾oz each, cut into strips • 1 red onion • 1 tbsp olive oil
• 1 red pepper, halved, deseeded and cut into strips • 6 shiitake mushrooms, sliced • 225g/8oz cherry
tomatoes, halved • ½ cucumber, peeled, deseeded and cut into julienne strips • 4 banana leaves
(optional) • 1 handful coriander leaves, chopped, to serve • 1 lime, cut into quarters, to serve
Dressing juice of 1 lime • 1 tbsp caster sugar • 1 garlic clove • 1 shallot • a pinch dried chilli flakes
• 2 tbsp Thai fish sauce • 1 tsp sesame oil

1 Put the ingredients for the dressing in the Vita-Mix machine and secure the 2-part lid. Select VARIABLE
  speed 1. Turn the machine on and gradually increase the speed to 10, then to HIGH. Run for 15 seconds
  until thoroughly combined. Put the chicken in a shallow dish and pour over 2 tablespoons of the dressing,
  then leave to marinate for 30 minutes. Transfer the rest of the dressing to a container and set aside.
2 Wash the Vita-Mix machine. Put the onion in the Vita-Mix machine and secure the 2–part lid. Select
  VARIABLE speed 1 and run for 3–4 seconds until finely chopped.
3 Heat the oil in a large non-stick frying pan over a medium-high heat. Add the chicken and onion and
  stir-fry for 6–7 minutes or until the chicken is cooked through. Leave to cool slightly, then transfer to
  a bowl. Add the red pepper, mushrooms, tomatoes and cucumber, pour over the remaining dressing
  and toss gently. Divide the salad onto the banana leaves, if using. Sprinkle over the coriander leaves
  and serve with the lime wedges.

HEALTH BENEFITS • Energizing • Immune-boosting • Stress-busting • High protein • Low carb
• Low cholesterol • Low saturated fat • Low calorie • Low kilojoule

Pot-Roasted Pheasant Stuffed with Chestnut & Bacon

SERVES 4 **PREPARATION TIME:** 40 minutes **VITA-MIX TIME:** 17 seconds
COOKING TIME: 50 minutes **SERVE WITH:** Roasted potatoes and steamed greens
STORAGE: Leftovers will keep in the fridge for up to 3 days. The sauce can be frozen
for up to 1 month. Defrost in the fridge before using.

1 shallot • 1 garlic clove • 4 slices streaky bacon • 3 tbsp olive oil • 3 tbsp Madeira
• 75g/2½oz chestnut mushrooms • 75g/2½oz cooked chestnuts • 2 flat-leaf parsley sprigs
• 50g/1¾oz butter, softened • 1 pheasant • 2 sprigs thyme

1 Heat the oven to 220°C/425°F/Gas 7. Put the shallot and garlic in the Vita-Mix machine and secure
   the 2-part lid. Select VARIABLE speed 1 and run for 6–7 seconds until finely chopped, using the tamper
   to push the mixture into the blades if necessary. Wash the Vita-Mix machine.
2 Cut 2 of the slices of bacon into small dice. Heat 1 tablespoon of the oil in a pan. Add the shallots,
   garlic and bacon and fry for 2 minutes, stirring occasionally, until golden brown. Add the Madeira
   and cook for a further 1 minute, then remove from the heat and transfer to a bowl.
3 Put the mushrooms, chestnuts and parsley in the Vita-Mix machine and secure the 2-part lid. Select
   VARIABLE speed 1 and run for 10 seconds until finely chopped, then transfer to the bowl with the bacon
   and shallot mixture. Add the butter and mix well.
4 Carefully ease the skin away from the breast meat of the pheasant. Spread the stuffing all over the
   breast meat and put the thyme sprigs into the cavity of the pheasant. Any additional stuffing can be
   cooked in a small dish separately, covered with foil.
5 Put the pheasant in a roasting tin and top with the remaining slices of bacon. Season with pepper
   and drizzle over the remaining oil.
6 Bake for 15 minutes, then reduce the oven temperature to 180°C/350°F/Gas 4. Bake for a further
   30–35 minutes or until cooked through, occasionally spooning any released juices over the pheasant
   during cooking. Remove from the oven and leave to rest for 10 minutes, then carve into thin slices
   and serve.

HEALTH BENEFITS • Energizing • Stress-busting • High protein • Low carb

Make this: *dairy-free by using a dairy- and seed-free margarine instead of butter. Make this sugar-free
by using apple juice instead of Madeira.*

SPECIAL OCCASIONS

161

Stuffed Roasted Quail with Wild Mushroom Cream

SERVES 4 **PREPARATION TIME:** 20 minutes **VITA-MIX TIME:** 4 minutes 20 seconds
COOKING TIME: 40 minutes **SERVE WITH:** Wilted baby spinach
STORAGE: The sauce can be prepared in advance and kept in the fridge for up to 2 days. Leftovers
will keep in the fridge for up to 2 days.

4 quail, boned • 4 slices of pancetta • 2 tbsp olive oil
Stuffing 30g/1oz ciabatta bread • 2 shallots • 1 garlic clove • 6 ready-to-eat prunes • ½ apple, cored
and quartered • 4 sage leaves • 1 flat-leaf parsley sprig • salt and freshly ground black pepper
Sauce 150ml/5fl oz chicken stock • 1 tbsp cornflour • 5 tbsp Madeira • 2 shallots • 1 garlic clove
• 100ml/3½fl oz double cream • 1 tbsp olive oil • 225g/8oz mixed wild mushrooms, halved or quartered
if large • 2 tbsp chopped flat-leaf parsley

1 To make the stuffing, select VARIABLE speed 2 and turn on the Vita-Mix machine. With the lid plug
   removed, put the ciabatta in the container blend for 4–5 seconds until coarse breadcrumbs form, using the
   tamper to push the bread into the blades. Turn the machine off and transfer the breadcrumbs to a bowl.
2 Turn the machine on again at VARIABLE speed 2 and add the shallots, garlic, prunes, apple, sage
   and parsley. Pulse on and off a few times until finely chopped, using the tamper to push the ingredients
   into the blades if necessary. Add the mixture to the breadcrumbs, season with salt and pepper and mix
   well. Wash the Vita-Mix machine.
3 Preheat the oven to 200°C/400°F/Gas 6. Spoon the stuffing into the centre of each quail and pull the skin
   around to enclose. Secure with string or use a cocktail stick or small metal skewer to secure the opening.
4 Wrap 1 slice of pancetta around the breast of each quail, then put them in an baking dish and brush with
   the oil. Bake for 30–35 minutes until golden brown and cooked through, spooning the released juices over
   the quail half way through the cooking time to baste.
5 While the quail is baking, make the sauce. Put the chicken stock in a saucepan over a medium-high heat
   and heat for 2 minutes until hot. Transfer to the Vita-Mix machine and add the cornflour, Madeira, shallots
   and garlic. Secure the 2-part lid and select VARIABLE speed 1. Turn the machine on and increase the speed
   to 10, then to HIGH. Run for 3–4 minutes until thickened. Turn to VARIABLE speed 3, remove the lid plug
   and slowly pour in the cream and run for 10 seconds until combined.
6 Heat the oil in a saucepan over a medium heat and fry the mushrooms for 2 minutes, stirring occasionally,
   until they begin to soften. Stir in the sauce and parsley and cook for a further 1–2 minutes, then season
   with salt and pepper and serve with the quail.

HEALTH BENEFITS • Energizing • Immune boosting • High protein • Low carb

Roast Beef & Yorkshire Puddings

SERVES 6–8 **PREPARATION TIME:** 15 minutes, plus at least 1 hour chilling
VITA-MIX TIME: 30 seconds **COOKING TIME** 1 hour 50 minutes
SERVE WITH: A leafy green salad and steamed broccoli and carrots
STORAGE: Yorkshire puddings are best eaten immediately, but you can prepare the batter the day before and keep it in the fridge until required. The beef will keep in the fridge for up to 3 days.

3kg/6lb 8oz boned and rolled beef • 2 tbsp olive oil • salt and freshly ground black pepper
Yorkshire puddings 115g/4oz plain flour • 4 eggs • 300ml/10½oz full-fat milk • 2 tbsp olive oil or beef dripping

1 To make the Yorkshire pudding batter, put the flour, eggs and milk in the Vita-Mix machine and secure the 2-part lid. Select VARIABLE speed 1. Turn the machine on and increase to 10, then to HIGH. Run for 30 seconds until smooth. Chill in the fridge for at least 1 hour, preferably overnight.
2 Preheat the oven to 200°C/400°F/Gas 6. Heat a large frying pan over a medium-high heat until hot. Rub the beef with the oil and season with salt and pepper. Add the beef to the hot pan and cook for 2 minutes on each side until browned.
3 Transfer the beef to a roasting tin and bake for 1 hour 20 minutes until golden brown. Remove from the oven, cover with foil and leave to rest for 20 minutes. Increase the oven temperature to 220°C/425°F/Gas 7. Thinly slice the beef.
4 Meanwhile, grease a 12-hole muffin tin with the oil or dripping and put the tin in the oven for 5 minutes until hot. Carefully pour the batter into the tins, filling the holes two-thirds full. Bake for 20 minutes until golden brown and risen, then open the oven door to let the steam escape and bake for a further 3–4 minutes until brown and crispy. Serve immediately with the roast beef.

HEALTH BENEFITS • Energizing • Stress-busting • High protein

Make this: gluten- and wheat-free by using an equal mixture of rice flour and tapioca flour in the puddings instead of plain flour.

Raspberry & Stem Ginger Tiramisu

SERVES 4 **VITA-MIX TIME:** 12 seconds **PREPARATION TIME:** 6 minutes, plus 1–2 hours chilling
STORAGE: Prepare in advance and chill for up to 1 day. Leftovers will keep in the fridge until the following day.

8 amaretti biscuits • 3 tbsp cold coffee • 1 tbsp amaretto liqueur • 1 piece preserved stem ginger
• 1 tbsp ginger syrup from bottled stem ginger • 250ml/9fl oz mascarpone cheese
• 250g/9oz crème fraîche • 350g/12oz raspberries • 3 tbsp icing sugar • cocoa powder, for dusting

1 Divide the biscuits into four dessert glasses. In a small bowl, mix together the coffee and amaretto liqueur and pour over the biscuits.
2 Put the ginger, ginger syrup, mascarpone and crème fraîche in the Vita-Mix machine and secure the 2-part lid. Select VARIABLE speed 1 and pulse on and off until the ginger is finely chopped and the mixture is well mixed, using the tamper to press the ginger into the blades. Wash the Vita-Mix machine.
3 Divide 200g/7oz of the raspberries into the four glasses on top of the biscuits. Spread the ginger cream over the raspberries, cover and chill for 1–2 hours.
4 Put the remaining raspberries and the icing sugar in the Vita-Mix machine and secure the 2-part lid. Select VARIABLE speed 1. Turn the machine on and increase the speed to 10. Run for 6–7 seconds until thick.
5 Drizzle a little of the sauce over each glass, dust with cocoa powder and serve immediately.

HEALTH BENEFITS • Energizing

Make this: gluten- and wheat-free by using gluten- and wheat-free amaretti biscuits.

Strawberry & Hazelnut Torte

SERVES 8 **PREPARATION TIME:** 10 minutes **VITA-MIX TIME:** 32 seconds
COOKING TIME: 40 minutes **STORAGE:** Leftovers will keep in the fridge for up to 3 days.
NOT SUITABLE FOR THE 32oz CONTAINER.

115g/4oz hazelnuts • 150g/5½oz soft brown sugar • 125g/4½oz plain flour • 60g/2¼oz butter
• 1 egg, beaten • 1 tsp baking powder • 150ml/5fl oz double cream • 175g/6oz strawberries, hulled
and finely chopped, plus extra, sliced, to serve • 2 tbsp strawberry jam

1 Preheat the oven to 180°C/350°F/Gas 4. Put the hazelnuts in the Vita-Mix machine and secure the
   2-part lid. Select VARIABLE speed 4 and run for 6–7 seconds until coarsely chopped. Turn the machine
   off. Remove the lid plug and add the sugar, flour and butter. Replace the lid plug and select VARIABLE
   speed 1. Turn the machine on and increase the speed to 10, then to HIGH. Run for 10–15 seconds or until
   the mixture resembles breadcrumbs, using the tamper to push the ingredients into the blades if necessary.
2 Put half the mixture in a 20cm/8in round springform tin. Press down with the back of a spoon until firm.
3 Put the egg, baking powder and cream in the Vita-Mix machine with the rest of the nut mixture. Select
   VARIABLE speed 1, then increase the speed to 10, then to HIGH. Run for 10 seconds until thick. Turn off
   the machine and stir in 100g/3½oz of the strawberries. Spoon the mixture over the base and bake for
   35–40 minutes until golden brown and firm. Remove from the oven and leave to cool completely.
4 When cool, top with the sliced strawberries. Melt the jam in a small pan over a low heat, then brush
   it over the strawberries to glaze. Chill until ready to serve.

HEALTH BENEFITS • Energizing • High protein • High fibre

Chocolate & Liqueur Panna Cotta

SERVES 4 **PREPARATION TIME:** 5 minutes, plus 4 hours chilling **VITA-MIX TIME:** 3 minutes 5 seconds
STORAGE: This will keep in the fridge for up to 3 days.

1 tsp olive oil, for greasing • 2 amaretti biscuits • 150g/5½oz plain chocolate • 125ml/4fl oz full-fat milk
• 2 tsp powdered gelatine • 2 tsp caster sugar • 200ml/7fl oz double cream • 2 tbsp amaretto liqueur

1 Lightly oil 4 x 150ml/5fl oz dariole moulds. Put the biscuits in the Vita-Mix machine and secure
   the 2-part lid. Select VARIABLE speed 3 and pulse on and off 2–3 times until they form coarse crumbs.
   Transfer to a bowl and set aside. Wash the Vita-Mix machine.
2 Put the chocolate in the Vita-Mix machine and secure the 2-part lid. Select VARIABLE speed 3 and run
   for about 10 seconds until coarsely chopped. Transfer to another bowl and set aside.
3 Put the milk in the Vita-Mix machine, sprinkle the gelatine over and leave to soak for 5 minutes, then
   add the sugar. Secure the 2-part lid and select VARIABLE speed 1. Turn the machine on and increase
   the speed to 10, then to HIGH. Run for 2 minutes until the milk is heated and the sugar and gelatine
   have dissolved. Remove the lid plug and add the chocolate. Replace the lid plug, then run on HIGH for
   30–40 seconds until the chocolate has melted and is mixed into the milk. Remove the lid plug and add
   the cream and liqueur. Replace the lid plug and run on HIGH for about 10 seconds to combine.
4 Pour the mixture into the dariole moulds and tap to remove any air bubbles. Cover and chill in the fridge
   for at least 4 hours.
5 When ready to serve, carefully dip the moulds into very hot water for 10 seconds, then turn them out
   on to individual serving plates. Sprinkle over the Amaretti crumbs and serve.

HEALTH BENEFITS • Energizing • High protein

Make this: vegetarian by using agar agar powder instead of gelatine. Make this gluten- and wheat-free
by using gluten- and wheat-free amaretti biscuits.

Chocolate Pecan Tart

SERVES 6 **PREPARATION TIME:** 15 minutes, plus 20 minutes chilling
VITA-MIX TIME: 1 minute 35 seconds **COOKING TIME:** 55 minutes
STORAGE: Leftovers will keep in the fridge for up to 3 days.

Pastry 300g/10½oz plain flour, plus extra for rolling the dough • 150g/5½oz butter • 3 tbsp caster sugar
Filling 150g/5½oz pecan halves • 3 eggs • 75g/2½oz soft brown sugar • 75g/2½oz chocolate
• 1 tbsp cornflour • 75g/2½oz butter, melted • 85g/3oz golden syrup • Icing sugar, for dusting

1 Heat the oven to 200°C/400°F/Gas 6. To make the pastry, put the flour in a bowl and, using your fingertips,
   rub in the butter until the mixture resembles fine breadcrumbs. Add the sugar and 1–2 tablespoons water
   and work together until a soft dough forms. Knead lightly then wrap in cling film and chill for 20 minutes.
2 On a lightly floured surface, roll out the pastry so that it is large enough to line a 23cm/9in flan tin.
   Line the pastry case with baking parchment and cover with baking beans. Bake blind in the oven for
   20 minutes, removing the beans and paper after 15 minutes. Remove from the oven and leave to cool
   slightly. Reduce the oven temperature to 180°C/350°F/Gas 4.
3 To make the filling, put half the pecans in the Vita-Mix machine and secure the 2-part lid. Select VARIABLE
   speed 1 and run for 4–5 seconds until lightly chopped. Sprinkle the nuts into the flan case.
4 Put the eggs and sugar in the Vita-Mix machine and secure the 2-part lid. Select VARIABLE speed 1. Turn
   the machine on and increase the speed to 10, then to HIGH. Run for 30 seconds until well mixed, then
   add the chocolate, cornflour, butter and golden syrup. Select VARIABLE speed 1. Turn the machine on and
   gradually increase the speed to 10, then to HIGH. Run for 1 minute until the chocolate has melted and
   the mixture has thickened slightly.
5 Pour the mixture into the flan case, sprinkle the remaining pecans over and bake for 30–35 minutes
   until risen and golden. Leave to cool for 5–10 minutes, then remove from the tin. Dust with a little icing
   sugar and serve.

HEALTH BENEFITS • Energizing

Babies & Toddlers

Polenta Pizzas

Cauliflower Cheese Purée

MAKES 4 portions **PREPARATION TIME**: 5 minutes **VITA-MIX TIME:** 10 seconds
COOKING TIME: 12 minutes
STORAGE: This can be frozen for up to 3 months. Defrost in the fridge before reheating.

150g/5½oz cauliflower, cut into florets • 30g/1oz Cheddar cheese • 4 tbsp crème fraîche

1 Put the cauliflower in a steamer and cook for 10–12 minutes or until soft.
2 Put the cheese in the Vita-Mix machine and secure the 2-part lid. Select VARIABLE speed 1 and run for
   5–6 seconds until finely chopped. Add the cauliflower and crème fraîche. Select VARIABLE speed 1. Turn
   the machine on and increase the speed to 3. Run for a few seconds until the mixture has reached the
   desired consistency, then serve.

HEALTH BENEFITS • Energizing • High fibre

Make this: *vegan by using soya cheese and yogurt instead of Cheddar and crème fraîche.*

Brown Rice & Apple Purée

MAKES 4 portions **PREPARATION TIME:** 5 minutes **VITA-MIX TIME:** 8 seconds
COOKING TIME: 25 minutes **STORAGE:** Leftovers will keep in the fridge for up to 2 days. Reheat over
a medium heat until hot and leave to cool slightly before serving. This can be frozen for up to 3 months.
Defrost in the fridge before reheating.

50g/1¾oz brown basmati rice • 1 apple, peeled, cored and chopped • 3 ready-to-eat dried dates
• a pinch cinnamon • 1 tbsp full-fat milk or natural yogurt (optional)

1 Put the rice in a sieve and rinse well under cold running water. Transfer to a saucepan and cover with
   water. Bring to the boil, then reduce the heat to low and simmer for 15 minutes until beginning
   to turn tender. Stir the apple and dates into the rice and simmer for a further 10 minutes, stirring
   occasionally, until the rice is soft, adding a little more water to the pan as needed.
2 Transfer the rice mixture to the Vita-Mix machine, add the cinnamon and secure the 2-part lid. Select
   VARIABLE speed 1. Turn the machine on and gradually increase the speed to 6. Run for 7–8 seconds until
   smooth or the mixture has reached the desired consistency.
3 Mix in the milk or yogurt, if using, and leave to cool slightly, then serve.

HEALTH BENEFITS • Energizing • Detoxifying • Immune-boosting • Stress-busting • High fibre
• Low cholesterol • Low saturated fat

Make this: *vegan by using fortified soya milk or yogurt instead of full-fat milk or natural yogurt,*
or by omitting the milk and yogurt completely.

Quinoa & Mixed Berry Purée

MAKES 4 portions **PREPARATION TIME:** 5 minutes **VITA-MIX TIME:** 3 minutes 40 seconds
STORAGE: This will keep in the fridge for up to 1 day. Reheat over a medium heat until hot and leave to cool slightly before serving. This can be frozen for up to 3 months. Defrost in the fridge before reheating.

30g/1oz raspberries • 30g/1oz blueberries • 500ml/17fl oz full-fat milk • 50g/1¾oz quinoa flakes

1 Wash the berries and drain well. Put the milk in the Vita-Mix machine and secure the 2-part lid. Select VARIABLE speed 3. Turn the machine on and increase the speed to 10, then to HIGH. Run for 2–3 minutes until heated through.
2 Remove the lid plug and add the berries and quinoa flakes. Replace the lid plug and select VARIABLE speed 3. Run for 10 seconds, then switch to HIGH and run for a further 30 seconds until the mixture forms a thick porridge.
3 Leave to cool to room temperature, then serve.

HEALTH BENEFITS • Energizing • Detoxifying • Immune-boosting • Anti-ageing • Stress-busting • High protein • High fibre

Make this: dairy-free by using fortified soya or rice milk instead of full-fat milk.

Apricot Lamb Burgers

MAKES 8–10 burgers **PREPARATION TIME:** 15 minutes, plus 30 minutes chilling
VITA-MIX TIME: 15 seconds **COOKING TIME:** 20 minutes
STORAGE: The uncooked burgers can be kept in the fridge for up to 1 day or frozen for up to 1 month. Defrost in the fridge before cooking. Leftovers will keep in the fridge until the following day.
SERVE WITH: Wholemeal rolls, salsa or coleslaw

75g/2½oz bread • 2 shallots • 1 garlic clove • 100g/3½oz ready-to-eat dried apricots
• 400g/14oz lamb mince • 1 egg • 2 tbsp olive oil

1 Put the bread in the Vita-Mix machine and secure the 2-part lid. Select VARIABLE speed 1 and run for 6–7 seconds until fine breadcrumbs form. Transfer to a plate and set aside.
2 Put the shallots, garlic and apricots in the Vita-Mix machine and secure the 2-part lid. Select VARIABLE speed 1 and run for 6–8 seconds until the mixture forms a paste, using the tamper to push the ingredients into the blades. Transfer to a bowl, add the lamb and mix thoroughly, then add the egg and enough breadcrumbs to make a stiff mixture.
3 Lightly wet your hands with water and divide the mixture into 8–10 small burgers of equal size. Put them on a plate, cover with cling film and chill for 30 minutes or until firm.
4 Preheat the grill to medium. Brush the burgers with the olive oil and put them on a baking sheet. Grill for 10 minutes on each side until cooked through, then serve.

HEALTH BENEFITS • Energizing • Immune-boosting • Stress-busting • High protein

Chocolate & Banana Custard Pudding

MAKES 4 portions **PREPARATION TIME:** 5 minutes, plus 15 minutes soaking and at least 30 minutes chilling **VITA-MIX TIME:** 30 seconds
STORAGE: Leftovers will keep in the fridge until the following day.

75g/2½oz ready-to-eat dried dates • 125ml/4fl oz full-fat milk • 2 bananas, peeled • 75g/2½oz almonds
• 60g/2¼oz chocolate chips

1 Put the dates in a heatproof bowl and cover with boiling water. Leave to soak for 15 minutes, then drain well.
2 Put the ingredients in the Vita-Mix machine in the order listed and secure the 2-part lid. Select VARIABLE speed 1. Turn the machine on and increase the speed to 10, then to HIGH. Run for 30 seconds until the chocolate chips have melted and combined with the rest of the ingredients, using the tamper to press the ingredients into the blades.
3 Divide the mixture into four bowls, cover with cling film and chill for at least 30 minutes, then serve.

HEALTH BENEFITS • Energizing • Stress-busting • High protein • High fibre

Pomegranate Jellies

MAKES 4 portions **PREPARATION TIME:** 10 minutes, plus 4 hours chilling
VITA-MIX TIME: 2 minutes 30 seconds **STORAGE:** This can be kept in the fridge for up to 2 days.
IF USING THE 32oz CONTAINER: Halve the quantities.

5 pomegranates, halved • 1 orange, peeled • 3 tsp powdered gelatine
• crème fraîche or natural yogurt, to serve

1 Hold each pomegranate half over a bowl and bash with a wooden spoon to release the seeds.
  Reserve 4 tablespoons of the seeds and put the remaining seeds and any juice from the pomegranates
  in the Vita-Mix machine. Secure the 2-part lid and select VARIABLE speed 1. Turn on the machine and
  increase the speed to 10, then to HIGH. Run for 20 seconds to extract the juice, then strain the juice
  through a sieve into a bowl.
2 Put the orange in the Vita-Mix machine and secure the 2-part lid. Select VARIABLE speed 6 and run for
  10 seconds until a thick juice forms, then add to the bowl with the pomegranate juice.
3 Add the gelatine to the juice and leave to soak for 5 minutes until soft, then pour the mixture into the
  Vita-Mix and secure the 2-part lid. Select VARIABLE speed 1. Turn the machine on and increase the speed
  to 10, then to HIGH. Run for 2 minutes until heated through and the gelatine has dissolved. Pour the juice
  into glasses or moulds and chill in the fridge for 4 hours until set. Top with crème fraîche or yogurt, sprinkle
  with the reserved pomegranate seeds and serve.

HEALTH BENEFITS • Energizing • Detoxifying • Immune-boosting • Anti-ageing • Stress-busting
• Weight-shifting • Low cholesterol • Low saturated fat • Low calorie • Low kilojoule

Make this: *vegetarian or vegan by using agar agar powder instead of gelatine.*

Feta Cheese & Cucumber Mash with Grilled Pitta Chips

SERVES 4 **PREPARATION TIME:** 5 minutes **VITA-MIX TIME**: 9 seconds **COOKING TIME:** 4 minutes
STORAGE: The pitta chips can be made in advance and stored in an airtight container for up to 4 days. Leftover feta cheese and cucumber mash will keep in the fridge for up to 3 days.

½ small red onion • 6 basil leaves • 200g/7oz feta cheese • 6 cherry tomatoes • ½ cucumber, peeled, deseeded and diced • 1 tbsp lemon juice • 4 tbsp olive oil • 2 pitta breads • freshly ground black pepper

1 Preheat the grill to high. Put the onion and basil in the Vita-Mix machine and secure the 2-part lid. Select VARIABLE speed 1 and run for 4–5 seconds until finely chopped. Add the feta and cherry tomatoes. Select VARIABLE speed 1 and pulse on and off 3–4 times until coarsely chopped and chunky. Transfer to a bowl.
2 Add the cucumber and stir in the lemon juice and 2 tablespoons of the olive oil. Season with a little pepper.
3 Cut the pitta breads into triangles or strips. Brush with the remaining olive oil and put on a baking sheet. Grill for 3–4 minutes until golden and crispy. Serve with the feta cheese and cucumber mash.

HEALTH BENEFITS • Energizing • Stress-busting • High protein

Make this: *citrus-free by omitting the lemon juice.*

Sweet Potato Gnocchi
with Four-Cheese & Onion Sauce

SERVES 4–6 **PREPARATION TIME:** 15 minutes, plus 15 minutes chilling **VITA-MIX TIME:** 17 seconds
COOKING TIME: 1 hour 5 minutes **STORAGE:** Leftovers will keep in the fridge for up to 2 days.

2 sweet potatoes • a pinch nutmeg • 1 egg yolk • 2–4 tbsp plain flour, plus extra for rolling the dough
and dusting • freshly ground black pepper
Sauce 4 spring onions • 1 flat-leaf parsley sprig • 150g/5½oz ricotta cheese • 50g/1¾oz Cheddar cheese
• 250g/9oz mascarpone cheese • 4 tbsp grated Parmesan cheese

1 To make the gnocchi, preheat the oven to 220°C/425°F/Gas 7. Put the sweet potatoes on a baking tray
and bake for 45 minutes until soft. Leave to cool slightly, then peel away and discard the skin.
2 Put the sweet potatoes in the Vita-Mix machine. Add the nutmeg and egg yolk, season with pepper and
secure the 2-part lid. Select VARIABLE speed 1, turn the machine on and increase the speed to 6. Run or
6–7 seconds until a thick purée forms and transfer to a bowl. Stir in enough of the flour to bring the
mixture together. Wash the Vita-Mix machine. Line a baking sheet with baking parchment; dust with flour.
3 Divide the mixture in half and, on a floured surface, roll each half into a long sausage shape. Cut into
2.5cm/1in pieces and put them on the baking sheet. Chill for 15 minutes.
4 Put all the ingredients for the sauce, except the Parmesan cheese, in the Vita-Mix machine and secure
the 2-part lid. Select VARIABLE speed 1. Turn the machine on and gradually increase the speed to 6. Run
for 8–10 seconds until thoroughly combined, using the tamper to press the cheese into the blades. Put
the mixture in a pan over a low heat and gently warm through until the cheese has melted.
5 Preheat the grill to high. Bring a large pan of water to the boil. Working in batches, add the gnocchi
and cook for 3–4 minutes or until they float. Remove from the water using a slotted spoon and drain
in a colander, then transfer to a baking dish. Pour over the sauce and mix gently, then sprinkle over the
Parmesan. Grill for 2–3 minutes until golden and bubbling, then serve.

HEALTH BENEFITS • Energizing • High protein

Lentil & Bean Chilli
with Cornmeal Topping

SERVES 4–6 **PREPARATION TIME:** 15 minutes **VITA-MIX TIME:** 1 minute 34 seconds
COOKING TIME: 45 minutes **STORAGE:** Leftovers will keep in the fridge for up to 3 days

1 onion • 1 garlic clove • 1 carrot, peeled • 300g/10½oz plum tomatoes • 2 tbsp tomato purée
• 2 flat-leaf parsley sprigs • 1 tbsp olive oil • 1 red pepper, halved, deseeded and cut into chunks
• a dash of Tabasco sauce • ½ tsp ground cumin • ½ tsp ground coriander • 150g/5½oz red lentils
• 400g/14oz tinned red kidney beans, drained and rinsed • 4 tbsp grated Parmesan cheese
Topping 185ml/6fl oz natural yogurt or buttermilk • 1 egg • 1 tbsp olive oil • 150g/5½oz fine cornmeal
• 2 tsp gluten-free baking powder • ½ tsp salt

1 Preheat the oven to 180°C/350°F/Gas 4. Put the onion, garlic and carrot in the Vita-Mix machine and
secure the 2-part lid. Select VARIABLE speed 1 and run for 3–4 seconds until coarsely chopped, then
transfer the mixture to a bowl.
2 Put the tomatoes, tomato purée and parsley in the Vita-Mix machine and secure the 2-part lid. Select
VARIABLE speed 1. Turn the machine on and increase the speed to 10, then to HIGH. Run for 30 seconds
until the mixture forms a sauce.
3 Heat the oil in a large casserole dish over a medium-high heat. Add the onion mixture, red pepper, Tabasco
sauce, cumin and coriander and cook for 1 minute, stirring. Add the lentils, kidney beans and sauce and
simmer for 15 minutes, stirring occasionally, until the lentils are tender. Add a little water if the mixture
becomes too dry. Wash the Vita-Mix machine.
4 Put the ingredients for the topping in the Vita-Mix machine in the order listed. Secure the 2-part lid and
select VARIABLE speed 1. Turn the machine on and gradually increase the speed to 10, then to HIGH. Run
for 1 minute, using the tamper to press the ingredients into the blades. Spoon this over the beans, sprinkle
with the Parmesan and bake for 30 minutes until golden. Leave to stand for 5 minutes, then serve.

HEALTH BENEFITS • Energizing • Immune-boosting • Stress-busting • High protein • High fibre

Puff Pastry Cod Parcels with Lemon & Herb Sauce

SERVES 4 **PREPARATION TIME:** 10 minutes, plus 15 minutes marinating **VITA-MIX TIME:** 4 minutes
COOKING TIME: 25 minutes **STORAGE:** The fish parcels and sauce will keep in the fridge for up to 2 days. The sauce can be prepared a day in advance and reheated when required.

4 skinless cod fillets, about 100g/3½oz each • 1 tbsp lemon juice • zest of 1 lemon
• plain flour, for rolling the pastry • 500g/1lb 2oz puff pastry • 1 egg, beaten
Sauce: 240g/8¾oz crème fraîche • 1 shallot • 2 tarragon sprigs • 1 lemon, peeled
• 2 tsp cornflour • 1 tbsp honey

1 Put the cod fillets in a shallow container and sprinkle over the lemon juice and zest. Leave to marinate for 15 minutes, then drain and pat dry with kitchen towel.
2 Preheat the oven to 200°C/400°F/Gas 6. On a lightly floured surface, roll out the pastry and, using a sharp knife, cut out 4 circles, each about 20cm/8in in diameter or large enough to enclose the fillets.
3 Put 1 cod fillet in the centre of each pastry circle. Brush the edges with the egg and fold the sides over so they meet in the middle. Pinch the edges together firmly to seal.
4 Put the parcels on a baking sheet and brush all over with beaten egg. Bake for 20–25 minutes until golden brown. While the parcels are baking, put the ingredients for the sauce in the Vita-Mix machine in the order listed and secure the 2-part lid. Select VARIABLE speed 1. Turn the machine on and increase the speed to 10, then to HIGH. Run for 3–4 minutes until hot and steaming.
5 Serve the parcels with the lemon and herb sauce.

HEALTH BENEFITS • Energizing • Stress-busting • High protein

Mini Meatballs with Tomato Sauce

SERVES 4–6 **PREPARATION TIME:** 15 minutes **VITA-MIX TIME:** 2 minutes 13 seconds
COOKING TIME: 40 minutes **SERVE WITH:** Pasta, such as penne, fusilli or spaghetti
STORAGE: Leftovers will keep in the fridge for up to 2 days.

Meatballs: 60g/2¼oz bread • 1 red onion • ½ red pepper, deseeded • 1 garlic clove • 50g/1lb pork mince
• 1 egg, beaten • 1 tbsp olive oil
Sauce: 1 onion • 1 garlic clove • 1 carrot • 1 red pepper, halved and deseeded • 3 tbsp olive oil
• 350g/12oz plum tomatoes • 1 tbsp tomato purée • 1 tbsp balsamic vinegar • 2–3 tbsp apple juice

1 To make the meatballs, put the bread in the Vita-Mix machine and secure the 2-part lid. Select VARIABLE speed 1 and run for 6–7 seconds until fine breadcrumbs form. Transfer to a small bowl and set aside.
2 Put the onion, red pepper and garlic in the Vita-Mix machine and secure the 2-part lid. Select VARIABLE speed 1 and run for 5–6 seconds until finely chopped. Transfer the mixture to a bowl and add the pork, egg and enough of the breadcrumbs to bring the mixture together, then roll the mixture into 15–18 small balls of equal size. Wash the Vita-Mix machine.
3 Heat the oil in a frying pan over a medium heat. Working in batches, fry the meatballs for 5 minutes, turning occasionally, until golden brown. Transfer to a plate and set aside.
4 Put the ingredients for the sauce in the Vita-Mix machine and secure the 2-part lid. Select VARIABLE speed 1. Turn the machine on and increase the speed to 10, then to HIGH. Run for 2 minutes until hot.
5 Pour the sauce into a baking dish large enough to hold the meatballs in a single layer. Put the meatballs over the sauce, cover loosely with foil and bake for 30 minutes until cooked through. Serve hot.

HEALTH BENEFITS • Energizing • Immune-boosting • Stress-busting • High protein
• High fibre • Low carb

Make this: *wheat-free by using oatmeal instead of bread; make it gluten- and wheat-free by using wheat- and gluten-free bread.*

Creamy Pork Korma

SERVES 4 **PREPARATION TIME:** 10 minutes **VITA-MIX TIME:** 15 seconds
COOKING TIME: 20 minutes **SERVE WITH:** Wilted greens and basmati rice or naan bread
STORAGE: Leftovers will keep in the fridge for up to 2 days.

1cm/½in piece root ginger, peeled • 1 garlic clove • 1 onion • 2 coriander sprigs • 1 tbsp olive oil
• 1 tsp garam masala • 400g/14oz pork fillet, diced • 30g/1oz whole almonds • 125ml/4fl oz chicken
stock • 5 tbsp crème fraîche • 2 tbsp toasted flaked almonds • 2 tbsp chopped coriander leaves
• freshly ground black pepper

1 Put the ginger, garlic, onion, coriander sprigs and 1 tbsp water in the Vita-Mix machine and secure
  the 2-part lid. Select VARIABLE speed 1 and run for 6 seconds until the mixture forms a paste.
2 Heat the oil in a non-stick frying pan over a medium heat. Add the onion paste and garam masala
  and cook, stirring, for 1 minute. Add the pork and continue to cook for 3–4 minutes until the pork
  begins to brown. Wash the Vita-Mix machine.
3 Put the whole almonds in the Vita-Mix machine and secure the 2-part lid. Select VARIABLE speed 1.
  Turn the machine on and increase the speed to 6. Run for 3–4 seconds until finely ground. Add the
  stock and crème fraîche and run for 5 seconds to combine.
4 Add the cream sauce to the pork and simmer, covered, for 15 minutes until the pork is cooked
  through. Season with pepper, sprinkle over the flaked almonds and coriander and serve.

HEALTH BENEFITS • Energizing • Stress-busting • High protein • Low carb

Carrot & Raisin Muffins

MAKES 10 muffins **PREPARATION TIME:** 10 minutes **VITA-MIX TIME:** 1 minute 7 seconds
COOKING TIME: 25 minutes **STORAGE:** These can be kept in an airtight container in the fridge
for up to 5 days or frozen for up to 1 month.

150ml/5fl oz light olive oil, plus extra for greasing • 100g/3½oz carrots, peeled • 100g/3½oz raisins
• 1 tsp mixed spice • 1 tsp ground cinnamon • 200g/7oz self-raising flour • ½ tsp bicarbonate of soda
• 2 eggs • 150g/5½oz caster sugar

1 Preheat the oven to 180°C/350°F/Gas 4 and lightly grease 10 holes of a 12-hole muffin tin. Put the carrots
 in the Vita-Mix machine and secure the 2-part lid. Select VARIABLE speed 1. Turn the machine on and
 increase the speed to 3. Run for 6–7 seconds until very finely chopped, using the tamper to press the
 carrots into the blades.
2 Transfer the carrots to a bowl and stir in the raisins, spices, flour and bicarbonate of soda. Wash the
 Vita-Mix machine.
3 Put the eggs, oil and sugar in the Vita-Mix machine and secure the 2-part lid. Select VARIABLE speed 1.
 Turn the machine on and increase the speed to 10, then to HIGH. Run for 1 minute until thick and creamy.
4 Add the egg mixture to the carrots and gently mix together. Spoon the mixture into the muffin tin.
5 Bake for 20–25 minutes until golden brown. Transfer to a wire rack to cool, then serve.

HEALTH BENEFITS • Energizing • Immune-boosting • Stress-busting • High fibre • Low cholesterol
• Low saturated fat

Apricot & Orange Fool

SERVES 4–6 **PREPARATION TIME:** 5 minutes **VITA-MIX TIME:** 50 seconds **COOKING TIME:** 3 minutes
STORAGE: This can be made in advance and kept in the fridge for up to 2 days.

3 oranges, peeled • 125g/4½oz dried apricots • 300ml/10½fl oz Greek yogurt
• 2 ready-to-eat dried apricots, finely chopped, to serve

1 Put the oranges in the Vita-Mix machine and secure the 2-part lid. Select VARIABLE speed 1. Turn the machine on and increase the speed to 10, then to HIGH. Run for 20 seconds until a thick juice forms.
2 Pour the juice into a pan, add the dried apricots and simmer over a medium-low heat for 2–3 minutes until the apricots have softened. Remove from the heat and leave to cool slightly.
3 Transfer the apricot and orange mixture to the Vita-Mix machine and secure the 2-part lid. Select VARIABLE speed 6 and run for 10–15 seconds until the mixture forms a thick purée. Set aside 4 tablespoons of the purée, then add the yogurt to the Vita-Mix machine and secure the 2-part lid. Select VARIABLE speed 6. Turn the machine on and run for 10–15 seconds until thoroughly mixed. Divide the mixture into four bowls or glasses. Drizzle over the remaining apricot purée, top with the chopped apricots and serve.

HEALTH BENEFITS • Energizing • Immune boosting • Anti-ageing • Stress-busting • High fibre

Make this: vegan and dairy-free by using soya yogurt instead of natural yogurt. Make this lower in saturated fat by using reduced-fat Greek yogurt.

Raw Honey Halva

MAKES 4–6 portions **PREPARATION TIME:** 5 minutes, plus at least 1 hour chilling
VITA-MIX TIME: 27 seconds **STORAGE:** This will keep in the fridge for up to 1 week.

oil, for greasing • 150g/5½oz almonds • 225g/8oz tahini • 125g/4½oz ready-to-eat dried dates
• 3 tbsp honey

1 Lightly grease a 20 x 25cm/8 x 10in baking tray with oil. Put the almonds in the Vita-Mix machine and secure the 2-part lid. Select VARIABLE speed 1. Turn the machine on and increase the speed to 6. Run for 6–7 seconds until finely ground. Add the tahini, dates and honey and secure the 2-part lid.
2 Select VARIABLE speed 1, turn the machine on and gradually increase the speed to 10, then to HIGH. Run for 10–20 seconds until the mixture forms a soft paste, using the tamper to press the mixture into the blades and stopping occasionally to scrape the mixture from the sides of the container.
3 Spread the mixture into the baking tray, cover with cling film and chill for at least 1 hour until slightly firm. Cut into squares and serve.

HEALTH BENEFITS • Energizing • Immune-boosting • Stress-busting • High protein • High fibre
• Low cholesterol • Low saturated fat

Make this: vegan by using date syrup or agave nectar instead of honey.

1